I0472051

DARK MATTER MECHANICS:

MEMORY, MIND AND CONSCIOUSNESS

By Allen Prince

FIRST EDITION

ISDN: 9781094738833

Independently Published

TABLE OF CONTENTS

PREFACE

The cover of this book is a depiction of the topic of Dark Matter Mechanics series how the vacuum performs work in a way that science has completely overlooked due to its presumption of empty vacuum, a false presumption that has been honored for more than one hundred years as a convenience or abstraction of reality. The cover depicts a molecule of water with vacuum gradients, the envelopes, surrounding the atoms and another surrounding the molecule itself where the red regions are comprised of larger particles than those comprising the blue regions to form a gradient. Electrons are held close their respective nuclear protons in the core and none are in orbit.

The molecule of water is the simplest and most common molecule in which the bonds between Oxygen and two Hydrogen atoms are depicted running from the protons in the core. Lines of force are structures in the vacuum that hold the electrons and run from the protons that together with those of other atoms form the magnetic field. The image is contrary to theory holding that the vacuum is empty and that electrons are in orbit, though they will when the atom spins if emitting waves.

The red and blue structure in the cover image represents the gradient envelope that all particles possess where the red represents larger vacuum particles in the gradient and blue represent vacuum particles that are smaller the closer they are to the boundary.

The bond is illustrated as a magnetic line of force between a proton in the outer shell of the nucleus and an empty slot in the nucleus of the outer shell of Oxygen. The line of force from the outer shell protons can lengthen when waves inject vacuum material into the proton envelope or shorten when material is lost by emission of electromagnetic waves allowing the dual personality of the water molecule able to behave as a weak acid or a weak base allowing Hydrogen to move farther away.

Each proton in the nucleus is ordered into shells that are now being erroneously being attributed to electron shells alone in orbits. The electrons are contained in their own envelope or magnetic field

4

securely within the proton magnetic envelope. It is unlikely that electrons are ever removed from the proton envelope as electric current or to change the charge of the atom though they may move away from the proton by expansion of the envelope size such as when electric current in the surrounding vacuum is under pressure.

While away, an electron from a metal atom may be captured by an empty slot of a nonmetal forming a bond holding the proton in the valence shell of a metal through the electron to at least two protons next to an empty slot in the valence shell of the nonmetal with various strengths. What is considered a weak ionic bond, the envelope of the proton of the metal can stretch to great lengths forming the appearance of severance from the proton envelope.

Current theory attributes behavior of the electron whenever a wave peak of vacuum occurs because a particle and a wave peak can have many of the same attributes by each having a high density at the center of the wave peak that behaves like a particle core and a gradient between it and the nearby troughs or the atmospheric density ahead and behind are gradients. The wave peak dissipates when the wave is forced into a fixed location, said to have no rest mass as is the photon.

In theory, the bond is between the electrons but here the electrons are retained in the proton envelope, obviously for the Hydrogen but not obvious for the Oxygen, a nonmetal with empty slots in the outer valence shell. The electron is confined in its proton envelope and bonds are between protons and protons in the nuclei, all of which is more fully set out in the section entitled ATOMS herein.

A theory in theoretical physics establishes a proof of a discovery basically in three parts. A mathematical representation of a behavior that the theory is to prove, construction of a model that illustrates the particular parts of the mathematics to be addressed and a general discussion of the discovery and of its importance relative to past discoveries. The proof need not, and invariably does not, have any evidence of causation. Any discussion about causation may exist in an informal comment that plays no part in the proof.

It is the purpose of this series, Dark Matter Mechanics, to prove there is causation for the theories in which a valid representation of behavior has been established and not necessarily to show a different behavior. The series is to supplement theory wherever possible but understanding the mechanics of material vacuum allows treatment not addressed by theorists for failure to establish causation, a property that is invariably avoided but is an important observable element of physics and to a mechanical universe. Many physicists have commented on the possibility that the vacuum is a material substance and must be, for that reason, comprised of particles.

Most of the mechanics of a molecular gas is understood and its ability to form solids and liquids can all be understood in terms of mechanical contact. Molecules, like the atoms, all possess a gravitation field argued herein to be a surrounding gradient, a vacuum structure that allows molecular gas to interact, whereas without the structures, the probability that they can interact is small to nil due to the small size of the molecules.

Mechanical contact is the primary law of mechanics and the gradients provide chain of contacts that makes the behavior mechanical. The particles of vacuum must comprise a medium in which particles are of all sizes allow free movement with no fraction whatsoever, mistakable as empty space without any empty space whatsoever.

Describing how the vacuum must be constructed as a particle medium and the structures it must be able to form and the mechanical causation of behavior that can be undertaken is discussed herein in the section entitled VACUUM but a more complete discussion is undertaken in the previously published "DARK MATTER MECHANICS: An Introduction to a Vacuum Science" in paperback and ebook formats. In a material vacuum, ordinary compression waves form the basis of theoretical energy and particle gradients form the fields in which particles attract or repel each other, all of which is covered herein and more completely in the earlier volume.

Much of the same material is covered here, enough to describe how the vacuum should be able to store memories as images of events, suggested in the earlier publication and treated more thoroughly here in the section entitled MEMOTY. It is shown here that the empty vacuum presumption prevents the ability of theorists to conceive of the memory structures described herein. While some of the arguments herein may seem unlikely, the purpose here is to investigate every possible use of material vacuum to perform the processes of the brain in formation of memories and how it can be stored and addressed. Without material vacuum, the magnificence of the nervous system might never be understood.

The mind and mental functions, under the topic of cognition, is being studied by many in numerous fields of science resulting primarily in an exhaustive list of categorical types of behavior and memory that are products of the mind, perhaps best regarded as normal and abnormal human psychological analyses. Some memories are regarded as inheritances and others as learned behavior. It might be said that all types of memory are dependent on some mechanism that is in common and likely exists in the lower biological species, and, notwithstanding that, much has essentially remained theoretically inexplicable.

Biochemists might suggest that the number and size of molecular formations can account for the memory functions in the brain and nervous system, many of which are detectable, particularly within the nerve cells. Memories are inheritable, suggesting that DNA is involved and take advantage, perhaps, of the processes described herein. The the lives of insects and other lower lifeforms allow us to see very complex behaviors that can only be inherited, the most commonly cited is that of the the spider and its inherited memory of web design and construction.

Anatomists and histologists may argue that the nervous system within the brain is able to process memory and logic through formation of paths using the vast number of the nerve cells that have means of communication through reconnection and growing new connections of their dendrite synapses that branch in uncountable ways. The true process must be accountable for forming new memory and retention of the older thoughts and observations. Most prominent is the discovery of neural nets or logic networks in the gray matter of the CEREBREL CORTEX and other similar structures of the brain able to produce decisions based on a selection process.

Computer scientists have developed programs that mimic the neural networks that are found in the gray matter of the brain and find that the network is able to identify images and select from a set of possibilities or images that is appropriate for a given criteria where the number of layers better refines the choices.

The neural network is not well suited for storing the data from which choices are to be made though where the processes of the brain take place is not well understood and is addressed herein, storage of the possible choices is critical to the logic of the process. While it is conceivable storage may be taking place within the network.

Some sciences are able to trace the electrical impulses and passage of chemicals at the synapse where on nerve cell exchanges information with another. Information must be transmitted through the neural connections to the various parts of the brain where processes occur depending on where the traces persist. Complexity arises through psychological and physiological studies where mental processes involving behavior and mental states are studied.

The size of the brain has grown through the very slow processes of evolution noticed through the study of the lifeforms that preceded us and our brains today, understood as processes of the biochemistry of DNA traced through the animal kingdom. The gray matter of the brain comprises the neural networks that is thicker and larger than any other species and formed in more layers that enhance the ability of the network. The brain has more bodily functions and nuance than any other species largely accounting for its size and complexity.

The physical body responds to images and sounds as complete sets rather than single bits of information though in the digital age, we tend to think of a collection of bits that are put in order to form a character set from which information can then be constructed or will form an image with information about its structure. There are many sets of structures that serve the purposes of character sets or images but origins is likely learned and are set in the brain as units of knowledge about how to read it. These are naturally

11

occurring or traced to some original source being sent to a particular region of the cortex.

On the other hand, images and other stimuli that are randomly input into the brain with great frequency must be interpreted and responses determined, a process that is theoretically able to put quantum bits of information together before they can be recognized as completed information takes time not only to learn but to process. Light is a string of compression waves that may contain more information than expected but not time stamped unless seeking a memory with a date stamp. Memories must be stored by time in a last in last out stack.

The brainwaves and electrical communication are waves, that are ubiquitous, contain whole images and not the bits used by computers then the evolution of the species would be inevitable since the process is embedded in the physics of nature without an organ for interpreting the complexity required for putting bits and bytes together and the many parts and processes required for a single image. A single atom, strategically placed, could give memory ability a simple organism if the processes described here are correct.

If the brain receives entire images rather than bits of information, it would be a much more efficient means of mental process in whole chunks rather than putting bits of information in all the possible orders to find a meaning that then must require searches and selection among learned data arriving from outside the body.

The physical responses of the body have increased with the evolution of the species so that the brain and nervous system is devoted to communication with the various muscles or glands needed to respond to various stimuli. This increases demand simply because of the greater sophistication of the society and complex demands due to advances in the dexterity of the body in communication with the mind. Not only are the muscles excited, the memory system must be apprised of the behavior and where ganglia in the spinal cord are involved, the brain must be notified of its work.

Scientists have pondered and theorized in their own field of study regarding the behavior resulting from the supposed processes of the mind and consciousness, none have yet determined the mechanisms that cause the behavior. The purpose here is not to survey in depth all the possibilities but rather to investigate the possibility that rather then being a biological process, that there may be more fundamental processes involving physics, without the maths, that facilitates the work of mind and consciousness.

The purpose here is to suggest a yet to be proposed more primitive means for the mind to process memory and coordinate thoughts, completely overlooked due to the universally accepted presumption of empty vacuum, first established just over a century ago, which excludes the work of the vacuum by theoretical empty vacuum and is unavailable, even when the aether theory existed. The aether was conceived as a simple standing gas at best, able to communicate waves of light as the luminiferous aether but not conceived as having a role in the fundamental processes being described here. The vacuum should therefore never be referred to as the aether.

The vacuum is more likely to be much more complex than the aether perhaps evolving over an infinite period before the event that created our universe as shown in the previous volume under the titled BIG BANG. It may be so complex that much of the life functions evolved before the first appearance of an actual life form in terms of mechanisms. Our investigations into the physical sciences may just now be advanced enough to determine and unravel the complexity of the vacuum that could have made possible the evolution of life, mind and consciousness inevitable and investigations are even now being undertaken but results of those endeavors are not known to be similar to those herein addressed.

Physics is now reduced to being a field of observable behavior where causation comes into the equation when the sources of causes are observable. Theoretical physics uses the mathematical descriptions of behavior developed in physics where the causes are not readily observable such as the ordinary and common compression wave and gradients in the vacuum that are able to move bodies at the particle level so that they are likely the invisible energy objects that drive the universe..

The gradients around proton particles, the magnetic envelope, the smallest particles form the envelope boundaries and are the same for all the envelopes in a collection forming the common glue among all the particles in a structure. Structures are generally dependent on their inertial frame. The boundless gravitational field at some point coalesces around groups of gravitating bodies to enhance their strength over any of the fields of the contained objects, seen for molecules and even galaxies.

The proton envelope is the magnetic gradient where the largest particles of vacuum are closest to the proton and are gradually smaller as the boundary is reached. The boundary is a shell of the smallest particles around which a reverse gradient exists that tends to buoyantly force particles away from the boundary serving to protect the interior from random particles in the surrounding atmosphere. An electron floats buoyantly some short distance from the proton at a location that changes as waves of material are allowed to enter the envelope by means of momentum of the wave.

During creation of the higher elemental atoms, the proton of Hydrogen atoms are attached to other Hydrogen protons to form the nucleus by a durable bond causing a one to one ratio of electrons to the protons of the element as set out in the Periodic Table of Elements. This concept is quite different from current theories of the atom.

The protons, argued herein, are attached in shells with the outer shell being the valence shell of a predetermined count where chemical activity takes place. If the valence shell has only one or a few protons, listed at the left end of its row in the table, the element is a metal and if close to the right end of the row in the table the valence shell is close to being filled with electrons, the element is a nonmetal. The metal with its filled electron slots can react with a nonmetal by filling one of the empty slots of the nonmetal where bounded by two filled slots.

When the valence shell is completely filled, the chemical activity is prevented and the element is a noble gas and marks the end of a shell and the beginning of a next shell. If the next shell is the outer shell then it is the valence shell. The number of the row in the Table shows the number of shells that have been filled. There are two categories that may not fit this model, the Lanthanoids, Actinoids and Transition metals that are generally very common metals but are not specifically addressed herein. According to the mechanical model of vacuum, each of the elements are able to collect and store information as images.

The proton envelope shapes are distorted by the existence of neighboring protons and when covered by another shell, the envelope theoretically becomes inactive. The envelopes of protons are extended beyond the location of the electron forming the magnetic lines of force, or magnetic field, the strength of which is determined by the number of lines of force that exists where measured. The lines of force extend outward in length to the extent that the magnetic field can be measured.

The extended envelope is the line of force where

the structure is also a gradient where the center along the length is the largest vacuum particles and are smaller toward the outer surface of the extended envelope and from the base of the line to the end, a gradient also exists creating the force and causing captured elements or waves to traverse the extension toward the proton.

The difference between a magnetic envelope and the gravitational gradient is that the gravitational gradient extends outward without limit. The confinement of the magnetic gradient gives it the strength for a limited distance compared to the gravitational gradient that gradually becomes weaker over great distances.

Associated particles form a group gradient that is stronger than any of its participants by formation of an envelope which becomes a quantum entanglement channel of communication when participants are separated. When stretched, that is somewhat similar to the proton's line of force, but becomes comprised of the small boundary particles in which waves travel faster than in the larger particles that comprise the surrounding atmosphere of vacuum.

Theorists acknowledge existence of the behavior of quantum entanglement to the extent that one separated particle of a group seems aware of the state of its former associate but how it works has remained inexplicable. Obviously, due to the empty vacuum presumption, even though communication channels must be taking place. A great deal of evidence shows that communication is faster than light, claimed to violate the laws of physics. The vacuum in the stretched envelope becomes an information channel that becomes a different inertial frame compared to the surrounding vacuum atmosphere, as argued herein. The particles of vacuum are smaller and therefore need less energy of inertia and momentum allowing waves to propagate much faster than those outside the channel.

The investigation herein is to determine the possibilities if the memory locations are not due to connections of cells or growth of chemical molecules but rather exist as the wave structures in the vacuum that are stored within the proton envelope. The magnetic gradient around the proton and in the lines of force may capture waves and cause them to travel towards the proton core. A relativistic process that may compress by flattening larger particles and removing others buoyantly out of place, larger particles leaving only some of their small gradient particles as a means of compressing the waves. The brain must be able to address these memories to be the process of which we are very familiar. The line of force can act like an antenna in both collecting and emitting waves of information.

Another very convenient condition must exist regarding the waves of information, the former volume establishes that electrical current is movement of waves in the vacuum rather than movement of electrons. These waves may move in the surrounding vacuum of a wire circuit or through liquid and even solids. One nerve function could be to collect these waves from the atmosphere and redirect them into the long axons, identified as electrical current. This could be a process that exists throughout the brain and a property of the physics that enhances the evolutionary process as very simple mechanisms allowing waves to be converted as electricity in the circuits perhaps as images to notify muscles to react.

The work in this volume and that of the earlier volume is not intended to change or replace the work of theorists but rather are to augment the knowledge and the theories that already exist as behaviors and to show how those behaviors are mechanically possible.

The natural neural networks have been compared to the computer networks but in order for that to be true, the waves that the networks are examining must contain information about where the wave originates which is read by all nodes of the network and ignored by all that are not able to use the information. The lobes of the CEREBRUM, the large cap of the brain, and the CEREBELLUM, a structure containing even denser gray matter, many of which are set out in the section herein as ANATOMY addressing the anatomy of the brain and the lobes of the CEREBRUM. This is information that is addressed by certain functions pointed out herein, though freely available on many cites on the Internet.

It should be noted that all particles, no matter how large or small, have a gravity field and many have a magnetic field in which the same processes described here could be taking place. It was stated earlier that all the particles of a gradient field are atomistic with a gradient of much smaller particles than the gradient particles of a core particle and each is surrounded by an atmosphere of the smallest particles in the structure, a ubiquitous sea of small particles.

It could also be true that the vacuum of an inertial frame are normal to the inertial frame which distinguishes it from others in which that same type or category of particle is relatively different in size. This may be true when an inertial frame has undergone acceleration causing all particles to become larger, arguably including the particles of the vacuum and the particles that form gradients around all the atomistic particles in the inertial frame.

Within an inertial frame, all the particles are likely to be surrounded by the smallest particles in the inertial fame, the ubiquitous sea mentioned above, allowing all to communicate through it as a medium in which obviously much smaller waves may pass. These waves may not be detectable as brainwaves or as anything at all but could take part in the processes of the brain in ways that cannot be imagined. Waves in that medium would be passed to every particle in the inertial frame, whether it be an isolated channel such as between entangled particles or particles comprising the gradient field of some much larger core such as a proton.

A molecular sound wave can be destroyed by rebound as echoes by meeting a solid wall of some sort surrounding the source but it should be understood that a wave captured and stored in a proton envelope is only a small segment of perhaps a sphere of compressed vacuum material emitted some distance away without causing the wave to collapse, as theory suggests. It should be noted that these waves might be infinitely faster than any other in the system by being comprised of infinitely smaller particles if through a medium like that in an entangled channel.

The concept of infinitely variable sizes in the vacuum is discussed in greater detail in the previous volume, in the section entitled PARTICLES, and the brain may be able to utilize properties of infinitely small particles and their waves. It could be in this sort of material that memory is stored as a result of the relativistic changes that takes place after capture of a wave. The vacuum particles within the entangled channels may feed its small particles into the envelope to decompress the stored memory waves to allow them to be recognized in some logic process.

Electromagnet waves in the material vacuum are better understood as regular waves sent from an spinning or, as theory tells us, orbiting source with quantum waves sent out one after the other to form the familiar sinusoidal structure traveling through the vacuum all at the same rate of speed. While these cannot be particles as Einstein argued, rather they are emitted as spherical waves and seen as particles due to the small apertures of the sensing port or organ collecting a port sized section from the wave. What is collected will appear as a particle but for the temporary peak region with similar properties to a particle. Theory gives this away by the properties of the various particles, as being able to occupy the same space at the same time which is a property of waves.

Every particle of whatever size possesses a surrounding field of very much smaller particles with a boundary of the same size that comprises the ubiquitous sea, mentioned earlier, perhaps infinitely smaller. A wave is comprised of vacuum particles and is packed closer together in the peak region causing the core, or largest central core, of the particles to be closer together that gives the peak its momentum. The waves are emitted from the proton envelope or its line of force acting as an antenna which is from the same place that captured waves are stored, as argued herein.

In an infinite space, small buildings might have been constructed, though very doubtful, but a quantum wave may contain a large amount of information perhaps in the gradient fields. The wavelength of an electromagnet wave is the length between one hump in the structure to the next, very much unlike the wavelength of a single compression wave where it is the length between one peak density to the next. Brainwaves must be electromagnet waves since that is all that theory has knowledge.

Critical to understanding how memories are accessed, copied and restored as new memory is difficult to describe even using mechanical theory being used here. For now, waves of information are collected by all reservoirs so that communicating a need to other reservoirs is not required. This requires that every atom is able to collect information from their date of creation held deep near the beginning of the stack and not easily accessed, if possible at all. These are stored sequentially with time so that the location in the stack reveals the time that the memory is stored.

This subject matter is discussed further in the section entitled MEMORY and RECALL where various possible means area addressed. The hope here is to stimulate thoughts formerly not conceivable due to the mistaken presumption of empty vacuum with possibilities not yet addressed elsewhere. Not only knowledge must be updated but technology most also be updated, if possible.

VACUUM

P hysics has established as a matter of fact that all mass has associated with it a gravity field and some possess a magnetic field, an extreme form of the same type. Gravity is a force field that extends without limit though while losing its strength the further away it is tested. The magnetic fields are limited in distance but have greater local strength than gravity but is likely confined in a limiting boundary that concentrates the material within it. These two fields have no explanation in the only two sciences that have responsibilities in such matters other than that these fields are both associated with a mass or a collection of mass, which at the level of this discussion are particles.

Most scientists agree that the vacuum is in fact a medium of some sort requiring that it be a medium of particles. For the vacuum to contain a field, it must possess a property able to force other particles of mass to be attracted to each other while at the same time repelled from others. We are aware in common knowledge of such a condition in the known mediums of particles which is that of the gradient field of varying density. Two ways of creating such a gradient is to have varying sizes of particles or having varying particle count per unit volume such that particles touching an object with varying degrees of force at different locations on the object causing an imbalance in forces.

The earth's atmosphere is a gradient of molecules in which a lighter than air balloon will seek a location of equal density. Water at any depth is a density gradient that is denser depending on the pressures placed at any point by the weight of the water above. The gravity and magnetic gradients must be more like the atmosphere by having its particles larger nearest the mass and smaller ones further away from the core or nucleus of the atom as a natural state forming a gradient structure that reforms when deformed or disturbed.

Water is a medium of like molecules where the gradient is due to the density count of water particles pressed together by the extent of water above to increase the density of water at lower levels allowing a body to sink to a set depth depending on the density of the body able to reach a point in the varying density of the water that is equal in density, much like in the atmosphere though the atmosphere the different molecules change with density,

It is easy to conceive of a vacuum that possesses both properties. The vacuum must be comprised of a great variety of particles to create a gradient in constant pressure that is around a particle of mass. The denser region is due to larger particles nearest a central core or nucleus and less dense as they are gradually smaller with distance as the outer boundary is approached.

The common compression waves that we ordinarily experience in a medium of constant sized particles that are able to elastically deform and return to their normal shape. To create a greater density, they are pushed by neighboring particles from behind to flatten the gradient to allow more of them to fit in a space in the direction of the wave. After the peak has formed, it begins to decompress as the gradients return to their normal shape behind and to push against and flattening their neighboring particles ahead in creating a new wave peak. A wave is a traveling density in the vacuum where the particles move very little using the particles in its path. As the particles are flattened, they necessarily impinge on the space of their neighboring particles to their side.

It must be the case that in formation of the gradient, the larger particles migrate closer to the core until reaching a location of particles its own size or larger as they easily push through any smaller particles in their way. Smaller particles must allow them to pass since they would impart less resistance by having less inertia.

A particle that is in a location in a gradient that is not of like size, the surrounding particles must squeeze the particle out of its misfit location where the constant pressure in the vacuum, known to exist. A universe wide atmospheric vacuum pressure is the engine for this other properties of the vacuum.

Gradients must require a large assortment of sizes to form when the particles in the gradient also have gradient structures. The smaller particles in vacuum are necessary to provide infinite lubrication where a total lack of friction exists, a near or absolute infinite assortment of particles must exist in the vacuum where each can be found in their own structures while performing in perhaps many larger and more vast structures.

The particles of the vacuum are all surrounded by the gradient fields that is referred to herein as the atomistic particle and the structure itself is referred to as the envelope possessed by all particles because they all are known to possess a gravity field and more ore less extensive magnetic gradients like that of the

the proton of Hydrogen.

When a collection of particles join, they form a joint envelope for the gravity field surrounding the collection having a greater strength and size than the largest particle in the collection. Galaxies achieve their huge gravity fields from a joint envelope that is greater than the sum of the individual bodies within.

When the particles or bodies that have a joint envelope, they are known as being associated, and when separated, the joint envelope is stretched forming a means of communication between the separated, bodies known as a quantum entanglement. The stretched envelope is bounded by the smallest particles as the outer membrane of the gradient within the envelope can be refreshed while the larger particles nearest the center all down are less dense so the stretched envelope leaving the outer membrane of smaller particles as the sole particles of the stretched envelope are capable of sending waves at a greater velocity, a property known to exist as quantum entanglement.

In an empty vacuum, scientists have no choice but to find a substitute for the properties that a material vacuum is able to produce finding particles where waves are more likely. The particles of vacuum are all atomistic and therefore are deformable and immediately reform to their normal shape. A wave in the vacuum therefore easily forms a normal compression type wave where a wave peak is denser with larger vacuum particles made closer together than the trough region where a gradient is formed between the trough and peak able to attract and hold objects having density within that range. This type of wave is essentially inconceivable to scientists laboring under the presumption of empty vacuum. When a peak is noticed in the vacuum, it can easily be regarded as a particle.

In normal common waves, the particles move from their normal position until a neighbor pushes it to its envelope boundary where it pushes the next vacuum particle, all of which takes place in the vacuum that exists ahead of the wave. Electromagnetic waves are a much different phenomenon. The proton envelopes in the outer valence shell are inflated by waves meeting the membrane of the envelope and penetrating and when this happens, the envelope can eject quantum sized waves which must cause the atom to spin creating the familiar sinusoidal shape comprised of tiny photon sized wave peaks.

In theory, these waves or photon particles are emitted by electrons in orbit in the conventional model which in turn causes the sinusoidal structure that retains its shape traveling at the speed of light, seen in both descriptions of the atom. The wavelength of electromagnet waves is the length between the peaks which in turn is the location where the structure is farthest from normal. The pattern is formed of connected compression waves but theorists must regard them as photons because compression waves cannot form in empty space. These small waves have peaks that can penetrate the proton envelopes causing them to inflate.

Another proven fact regarding moving particles of all sizes, they are each accompanied by a wave as observed in experiments. These waves that are associated with moving particles are inexplicable to theorists since compression waves capable of the phenomenon are not possible in the presumed empty vacuum. The effects of these waves are theoretically undetermined but it is very likely that the waves are driving the particles held by the gradient between the low density trough and the high density peak.

If waves are driving the movement of particles then the energy of inertia of particle is likely in formation of the wave that is capable of initiating movement. More energy added to the wave becomes the energy of the momentum of the moving particle. The particles of the vacuum surrounding the particle to be moved are compressed by additional waves that are added with sufficient force to move the particle. This is an example of energy capable of moving an object and perhaps is an example of all forms of energy cited as the fundamental phenomenon created as the source of all that we know arising as the theoretical big bang forming the universe.

It is known that no contact is made between core particles, often referred to as due to the presence of their fields but referred to herein as their gradients that repel achieving the appearance of like poles of two bar magnets. The concept of magnetic forces is often questioned in view of the fact that it is known that a pole of a bar magnet cannot be separated from its opposite pole.

The electron within the proton envelope also has an envelope that may be affected by the influx of wave peak material but it is certain that the event will cause the location of the electron within the proton envelope due to changes in the buoyancy of the electron in the material. The wave peak able to enter the proton envelope is mostly larger vacuum particles that exist in the peak region of waves. This material will cause the electron to increase its distance from the proton.

MEMORY, MIND AND CONSCIOUSNESS

Quantum mechanics in the theory of orbiting electrons of the atom is described conventionally using the photon particle containing a quantum of energy and that one or more photon units of energy will cause an electron in orbit to jump to a new higher energy orbital. The model grew from studies of light affecting the energy of electrons in the atom.

In black body experiments, it was found that energy of light increases in quantum units giving rise to the quantum unit of energy being the smallest unit of energy that exists. Quantum mechanics is now regarded by most as a factual phenomenon where the quantum unit is the energy of the photon particle, thanks to Einstein. It is possible that this is an example of identifying wave peaks as particles as all that can exist in the empty vacuum are particles. Compression waves are inconceivable while honoring the presumed empty vacuum.

The magnetic field that surrounds the proton is a strong gradient field with the smallest particles forming the outer boundary encapsulating the magnetic gradient within. The largest particles are nearest the proton and the electron with its own magnetic gradient is contained therein located at a point that is dependent on the gradient in which it is suspended.

DARK MATTER MECHANICS

The boundary particles of the envelope generally prevent particles from entering the interior of the envelope unless they have the momentum of a wave, in which case the peak of the wave comprised of the largest particles in the surrounding vacuum will enter causing the envelope to inflate and change the gradient structure in the envelope causing the electron to move away from the proton particle in accordance with the quantum mechanical model.

Theorists describe the magnetic and gravitational fields in terms of behavior of objects of mass in a field. Motion of a body is described in terms of the energy to overcome inertia and further energy sufficient to drive the momentum in terms of mass and velocity or acceleration. In other words, the presumption of empty vacuum enables theorists to be able to avoid discovery of what could be causing the behavior and disparage the act of seeking causation as being unproductive or seeking to know something that cannot be understood.

The theoretical energy is mechanically the difference in pressures against a body sufficient to cause it to move so that adding pressure to the back of a body or reduction of pressure in front of a body would cause it to move forward. Both conditions are the means for movement when a body is in a gradient. A compression wave creates a density in vacuum where a reduction exists in a trough and an addition exists at some point as the peak is approached.

These waves have the energy to move objects from small particles to huge bodies being overlooked by theorists due to the empty vacuum presumption. Theorists are interested in proving a theory by describing a behavior mathematically accompanied by a model that illustrates the expressions in the theory with an explanation of the theory. The theory for energy was expressed in Einstein's famous expression as energy is equal to mass times velocity squared. Nothing is said about the mechanisms involved because they cannot exist in the presumed empty vacuum.

The gradient between the trough and peak of a wave is much like a gravitational or magnetic gradient able to grab and hold an object if the gradient is strong enough and not too strong. A wave behaves according to the laws of motion by continuing in a direction at the same velocity, at the speed of light unless burdened by a mass, and until meeting another force, generally against the body that is being moved in the form of another body driven by another wave.

The proton is responsible for the magnetic field that holds an electron but also for magnetic lines of force measured at a distance as an extension of its envelope. The line of force as an extension of the proton envelope can behave as an antenna for collecting and sending information. A gradient must exist in the line of force to exert its attraction properties but must also have a gradient with larger particles running down center to smaller boundary particles on the outside. This is the necessary construction of quantum entanglement between separated particles by stretching its group envelope.

The magnetic lines of force are the proton envelopes of the outer shell of the nucleus of the atom extending out as far as the magnetic field can be measured, past the location of the electron. It is the magnetic lines or force that continuously capture electromagnet waves which are driven toward the proton core where along the way they suffer enlargement and flattening of the particles, The largest of the particles are squeezed out and rise to form a new wave as a new electromagnetic wave which causes the atom to spin while emitting quantum sized compression waves that form the planar sinusoidal shaped electromagnetic wave.

Core particles come in all sizes from the particles in the vacuum of the smallest cores which is a paradox unless the sizes range is infinite. The atomistic structure is like that atmosphere of the planet where the largest molecules are closer to the surface and smaller near the outer realm. Lighter than air balloons exemplify buoyancy by rising to a specific location in the atmosphere of equal density.

When the core of an atomistic particle is larger than another, the difference is in the inner regions of the largest gradient allowing a region of similarity nearest and including the outer boundary. The difference is n not in outer region while the difference will be in the innermost regions leaving the outer regions the same facing the outer atmosphere while the size of the gradient field is increased. The outer regions of the gradient must be the same to allow them each to interact in the same way and in the space between the gradients of close neighboring particles being of small particles that are continuous between all particles in a given collection or possibly within an inertial frame. This material must be what is used in formation of the group envelope and is used in forming the quantum entangled channel of communication with few or no larger inner particles.

The same can be said for the sizes of planets throughout the universe where the vacuum nearest the surface of a very large planet is likely made of larger particles than those found here. As waves are generated close to the surface, such as those we can see for the color of the surface, the wave is modified as it leaves the inner regions and through the outer regions forming the waves of the same material meeting the outer atmosphere of our or any other planet.

When associated particles or groups separate from each other, it is the outer region that forms the quantum entanglement though they can be much larger than implied by the reference to the word "quantum" though perhaps not for different inertial frames, formed of small particles, due to possible differences in size of the smallest particles in each though that may possibly not be the case according to the theory of relativity, addressing differences in velocity. Quantum entanglement can be induced between photons that are separated as seen in experiments currently.

By this property, all particles in a collection arising from a common source may be connected by quantum entanglement, perhaps even all particles in the universe since all particles were once associated in the big bang though see the section entitled BIG BANG in the first volume of this series. Waves passing through an entangled communication are using smaller particles than in other regions in an inertial frame and a small particle possesses less inertia and starts and stops more quickly as needed in a wave. That is not to say that transmission of waves is the only property of quantum entangled channels. Generating a wave at one end will cause emission of material at the other.

If the big bang theory is correct then perhaps all the particles in the universe are to some extent a web of quantum entanglement. The waves that are formed within a quantum entangled tube will be made of the same particles that inhabit it so that it becomes a way to inject a set of smaller vacuum particles into a magnetic envelope in which ordinary wave injections are of larger particles that are perhaps images that are stored nearest the core of the atomistic particle. The subject is treated in the section entitled BRAIN herein.

Memory and thought processes may use inconceivable means in a theoretical universe presumed to be filled with empty space incapable of any processes whatsoever but for the fact that all the processes seem to be taking place in the vacuum. The "DARK MATTER MECHANICS" series seeks to discover the means that are likely available in a vacuum of infinitely variable sizes of particles comprising the vacuum causing the precise theoretical descriptions of behavior of theory.

ENTANGLEMENT

Entanglement was first coined to satisfy a mathematical problem in logic where everything should be described using the logic of mathematics. The problem is expressed in terms of the unknowability of some information when there is more than one possible result. It is expressed in the thought experiment proposed that is well known as the Schrodinger's cat experiment, in a famous thought experiment which in mathematics can be regarded as a theoretical paradox.

The classical description of the experiment is to place a hypothetical cat in a hypothetical box along with a hypothetical poison in a bottle that can be broken after the box is sealed when the cat decides to eat. After a given time and possibly after the poison has been released from the bottle, the theorists who addressed the question were attempting to address a problem in quantum mechanics where results are often ambiguous. They agreed that until the state of the cat is known, it may be regarded logically as both alive and dead at the same time as in quantum theory to satisfy the need for labeling the question whether the cat is alive or dead.

A real experiment involves separation of associated particles that have different states and the experiment as first addressed allows the particles to be separated and without knowing which state exists in either of the particles, testing one will cause the other to have the other state. While there is no mystery in that experiment proving only the persistence of the states when moved. The paradox occurs when one that is examined also causes its associate to also switch its state, the other will be found to be the other state even after the first is switched. Both of these experiments are referred to as examples of quantum entanglement. The first example is easy but not the other in which changing the state must be communicated to the other to allow it to switch its state.

Based on the latter of the two experiments in the preceding paragraph where there is an apparent communication demands a response even though the experiment seems to only know when a change occurred. Even that experiment is incomplete in that it is not allowed to examine for their states until finally examined and only the one time. There is some probability that the first was like the other before being changed without some assurance that they in fact were in different states before being changed or separated. This, because examining the state fixes the state of the particle examined but the experiments examine the results in terms of convincing probabilities. Still, the problem involves unknown states where possibilities are held in memory.

There can be no change of the state after looking since examining the state generally destroys the state unlike examining the life state of Schrodinger's cat and still regard it as possessing both states. The consensus is that no more information can be communicated than the unknown state that is changed remotely. Real experiments are being conducted confirming that true information is transferred after separation in unique ways as evidence of a channel of communication between separated objects.

Credible experiments have been proving that quantum entanglement exists and some have established that the change in results can be known before the fact of the execution and the experimenters claim the experiment establishes behavior in the future and to be able to foretell the future. The presumption of empty vacuum would forbid a presumption that an actual channel of communication exists between the entangled particles. To understand this problem, one must understand that the speed of light can differ from one inertial frame and another as viewed by a party outside of either inertial frame, as correctly stated by Einstein.

Because there are structures being proposed herein in the vacuum, there should be no surprise that an actual channel might exist for more purposes than a mere exchange of states. Some regard the statement that the speed of light is the fastest that light can travel which is not entirely true depending on the inertial frames and possibly their distance from each other. If the test equipment is in the same inertial frame and the communication is taking place, the speed of light will be tested as the theoretical variable having a constant value of c. If the equipment is external to the light being tested, the speed will vary and can in fact be tested to be faster than c. This is an explicable finding though is specifically stated in the special theory of relativity without addressing the state of the vacuum.

If an inertial frame is accelerated then an increase in the mass of particles will occur, validated in experimental accelerators with relativistic effects. It will take more energy for particles to move about and time will slow down as acceleration is increased and the speed of light will be reduced. While Einstein treated the vacuum as being empty, he failed to state the cause of the acceleration effects. If the vacuum in which the light is traveling becomes more massive, then the energy of inertia and momentum must increase illustrated in the equation relating mass and energy. Einstein explains the situation as changes in the inertial frame. While achieving a decrease in the mass of vacuum particles, it would cause light to travel faster and arrive at a point before expected, in the future.

It is likely that theorists are convinced that an entanglement allows no more than the state to be exchanged since quantum mechanics fails to allow more than the single quantum bit of information that places an orbiting electron in a new state a single orbital at a time, unlike the volume of information that the atom can hold in mechanical theory being used herein. No more than state is theoretically passed since there may be no experiment that can be devised that proves otherwise. There is another possibility that is not addressed herein, that as particles in the inertial frame get smaller, the waves travel faster so that there must be layers of vacuum as in the ubiquitous sea surrounding all particles in which light can travel even faster but no one can remove the instruments to measure the speed out of that environment.

The gravitational gradient for particles is extended

to more than a single particle as waves that are stronger and extends further than is measurable over a longer distance than that of any of the single particles can achieve. A collection of particles must form an envelope that is similar to the envelope of magnetic fields that creates a much steeper gravitational gradient inside the field.

Collections have gravity fields that are stronger than the strength of the largest particle in the collection. Gravity for the collection would be otherwise no more than the largest particle in the collection and have a drop in strength to an ineffectual level for each of the individuals in the collection. The collection will form a surrounding gradient with a boundary that is stronger than any in the collection due to the bound field and the forces of gravity are multiplied both in the strength and effective distance as seen for the galaxies of the universe and our own solar system acting as an inertial frame.

Other structures exist that are not force related but rather are related to communication as wave conduits. If two or more related particles are separated, the shared gravitational envelope becomes stretched to the extent that internal structure becomes comprised of the same smaller particles as the boundary resulting in an inertial frame that is different from that of the surroundings. This allows the tubular structures to become quantum entangled where the smaller particles conduct waves at a much faster rate due to their reduced inertial energies of smaller particles. Particles in waves must start and stop after moving a short distance at what must be faster than the speed of light.

Quantum entanglements may exist in a network between all separated particles within a confined space in which all the atoms and particles have been associated with all the others at some time in the past. For that reason, the concept must be well understood if the abilities of the brain are to be understood. Many, if not all, operations of the brain are conducted simultaneously and may not have a control function having a monitoring ability to keep them all in sync if virtually simultaneous.

Of course, a wave that is able to sweep across the brain surface will be read almost simultaneously by the logic network reaching some slightly before others farther away. In that case, quantum entanglement may have a part in many of the functions such as injecting into a region or envelope a set of its own small particles to dilute a compressed region. By the same token, the compression process may be to squeeze the smaller gradient particles out of the wave and into and entangled channel. Just because entanglement is an approved real state, that does not mean that it is well understood other than behavior, the sole work of theorists.

These smaller particles can be more compatible with each other forming yet another network that could be very difficult to imagine without some knowledge of the vacuum. Proton envelopes may be received and take part in some of the relativistic processes that must take place as waves travel toward the mass of the proton in an increasing gravity density of that gradient. If information is to travel in an entangled network at a rate faster than the light we are able to measure in our environment, waves may be much slower than waves in an entangled channel able to prepare recipients of the ordinary waves in advance of their arrival.

Because all particles have a gravity field and waves are generally spherical around the source so that a wave that contains information may well be stored in all the particles that exist inside the brain cavity, the skull. When a traveling spherical wave passes a particle capable of capturing it, only a small part of the spherical wave is captured and it is that part that is often mistaken for a particle. The waves that are in the brain cavity are waves generated by sensory organs of the body and transmitted as a wave, first as an electrical wave in a nerve fiber and then released as a brainwave in the other substances of the brain.

It is very likely that the reservoirs for memory are in the atoms that comprise the gray matter of the brain, perhaps everywhere that the wave passes over which is the entire area of the cortex material since the dendrites of the nerves in the gray matter generally face outward toward that cerebral spinal fluid. If that is the case, the needs for any communication between the various regions of the brain are in generally unnecessary.

A wave carrying important information would be virtually acted upon at the same time in parallel. The skin is a sensory organ that passes information of injury to the brain through the spinal cord and into brain cavity through the brainstem. From there, it is possible that all the regions of the brain receive the same information at the same time where analysis begins throughout the brain at the same time seeking a correct response.

BRAIN

The brain is comprised of a complex of structures and tissue types involved in sending and receiving stimulation from outside the brain and within. The primary parts of the brain are the CEREBRUM, the CEREBELLUM and the BRAINSTEM. The CEREBRUM is divided into the right and left halves, where in general each hemisphere directly serves the opposite side of the body but exchange functionality through a structure that lies between called the CORPUS CALLOSUM. The first two parts are together referred to herein as the CORTEX.

The often cited left side of the brain serves speech, comprehension, arithmetic and writing while the right side controls creativity, spatial ability, artistic and musical skills. Parts of these functions may be reversed for left hander individuals that comprise around eight percent of the population. Each hemisphere is divided into four lobes that are the

DARK MATTER MECHANICS

FRONTAL, TEMPORAL, PARIETAL and OCCIPITAL Lobes. These each have their own sets of functionality.

Much of the functionality of the structures and tissues of the brain have been discovered through various means, by direct stimulation where pain is not sensed in the brain so that patients are awake and can report the sensations being experienced as from elsewhere in the body or as memories of the past, and so on. Another means is through the electroencephalography (EEG) when a known sensation is introduced, the brainwaves are observed and recorded.

The main and permanent means of communication within the brain is through stimulation of nerve cells and through paths that are able to reach other parts of the brain. These paths theoretically can be either permanent or temporary branching of their short dendrites growing out of the nerve cell body or at the ends of the longer axons that may communicate with the rest of the body through the spinal cord. The brain is also able to secrete hormones that are spread about the body or brain through blood circulation that perform functions.

The EEG evidence is that stimulation of the brain

will trigger a storm of brainwaves that begin at the point of stimulation and then washes throughout the brain. It is argued herein that electricity is itself waves in the vacuum inside or outside of a circuit so that brainwaves are emissions at the dendrites of nerve cells after accepting the waves where they are stored or passed through the axon as an electrical pulse or as a wave containing information.

It is a mistaken theoretical view that electrical current is movement of electrons in a circuit which is very likely an artifact based on the equally mistaken presumption of empty vacuum and the need to point to a set of particles as the basis of current. Considering that electrons move very slowly through a circuit and there is very little chemical degradation when current is passed through a metal circuit, all of which negates electrons as electric current and supports current as vacuum waves in ample vacuum..

The fact is that the vacuum is ubiquitous and occupies virtually all of space with tiny bits of solid matter occupying negligible volume. Clearly, the atoms and their particles are under control of the vacuum. Theoretically, theorists honor the presumption of empty vacuum but if the vacuum is a material medium, as being argued herein, a great many properties attributed to it may become explicable and new properties discovered.

Theoretically, the vacuum is presumed to be empty space but there are properties of vacuum that tend to contravene the presumption. Before the nuclei of atoms were discovered using scatter patterns after metal foil was shot through with Alpha particles, it was found that particles that were not impeded by the nucleus, previously believed to be solid matter, were allowed to pass but were deflected indicating, theorists said, the existence of a field that was modeled after the poles of bar magnets. The Alpha particles were deflected away from the newly discovered nucleus much as like poles of bar magnets that repel.

In physics and chemistry alike use the model based on the bar magnet properties. The thought is due to the protons in both the nucleus and Alpha particles deemed to have like magnetic charges accounting for the apparent repulsion. As a model, there is nothing wrong since it does exhibit the modeled response since models are not deemed a representation of reality. The behavior of magnets and that of repulsion of particles are due to properties of the vacuum but neither is theoretically understood and especially inexplicable since the vacuum is presumed to be empty and devoid of matter.

MEMORY, MIND AND CONSCIOUSNESS

The magnetic model, like all models, was not the reality since, in reality, the poles of bar magnets cannot be separated from each other as being bipolar but the particles in the atom must be mono polar. Theorists could have determined that the regions outside of the nuclei are just as before, a material that is not absent but rather is penetrable but comprised of a gradient causing the deflection. It is this view that is argued to be the case herein. Similarly, the old model held that inactive electrons are embedded within the solid matter of the atoms while active electrons are located on the surface of atoms, all of which are supported by the Periodic Table of the Elements if the electrons on the surface represent the valence shell of the elements.

Furthermore, the atoms are theoretically comprised of a point positive magnet in the nucleus with electrons in orbit around the nucleus, argued herein are mechanically inoperable. Electrons in orbit in response to a point magnetic charge randomly in their orbits without being responsive to any one proton in the nucleus to avoid the randomness is more likely in a material vacuum as argued herein. The protons with their magnetic envelope are more likely each in control of its own electron residing in the nucleus in the shells now theoretically being the electrons in shells. All the theoretical properties of atoms with electrons in orbit are satisfied by protons and their electrons residing as

Hydrogen atoms.

The orbiting model is contrary to the needs of chemistry since the formation of bonds by the elements are not theoretically able to form by orbiting electrons or able to remain in orbit after a bond has been formed. More significantly in this discussion is that orbits are not able to retain information other than changes in orbitals due to the quantum mechanical theory only until emitted as a wave.

A mechanical model of the elements is somewhat different then the model of theory by providing a means for storing information in the wave being accepted while still emitting the waves that are known to occur. Possibly, the construction of atoms in the stars was by combining Hydrogen held together at the protons of the nucleus. This would allow the structure surrounding the proton of Hydrogen to hold its electron and reach out as the magnetic lines of force, as originally framed by Faraday. The lines of force can act as antenna for collecting waves and emitting them, as more completely discussed in the section herein entitled ATOMS.

The proton gradient envelope is able to accept energy of peak waves in the surrounding vacuum by their momentum, able to penetrate the boundary which moderates the location of the electron relative to the proton of each Hydrogen atom. These energy waves are created by means of the senses that accept waves from outside or from unspecific locations in the brain. The theoretical electrons in orbit accept energy waves from the vacuum that elevates the orbit until emitted later according to quantum mechanics but Hydrogen has a region in which endless amounts of waves can be chronologically stored, perhaps in compressed form due to relativistic properties as the wave is sent toward the proton and a means of emitting waves through its extended envelope designated a line of force.

Instead of electrons in orbit accepting energy waves, the proton and electron gradients accept the energy waves causing the electron to buoyantly change its location. The energy waves coming from many directions in sequence can enter the envelope to be stored as intact images while energy emissions from the envelope must cause the atom to spin while emitting electromagnetic waves of light to satisfy the theoretical means of electromagnetic wave formations. Current theory has electrons emitting photons as it travels through its orbit causing its characteristic sinusoidal shape now theoretically emitted by electrons in orbit. It is unclear where the emissions are stored before emitting their waves. The quantum elements of the wave are small compression waves as theory describes.

There is controversy regarding the means for storing memory of information being detected from outside the brain and internal thoughts generated from within the brain, discussed in greater detail in the chapter on MEMORY. For theorists, this concept is inconceivable for those who are bound to honor the empty vacuum presumption. The forgoing is mechanical theory where vacuum gradients and compression waves are only possible in a vacuum comprised of particles of vacuum, discussed further in the chapter on VACUUM.

Particles are known to form gravitational and some have magnetic force fields surrounding detectable particles or objects of mass and likely all particles regardless of their detectability. Having the ability to initiate waves has been, in theory, imprecise while the particles of vacuum are able to form compression waves and to comprise electrical current in closed circuits and create friction in a constricted circuit to generate heat. Vacuum waves are the energy of theoretical physics where density variation between the peak and troughs of the waves is a gradient field able to capture any particle with density within the range. Gradients surrounding particles as gravity or magnetic fields are essentially sources of energy as being able to buoyantly induce motion, the definition of energy. The gradient between the peak and trough not only causes movement toward the peak or trough but if that occurs, the wave could move the particle as the wave travels through space.

There is experimental evidence, aside from the theoretical basis for duality of particles arising out of quantum mechanics that waves associate with moving particles of all sizes that are argued herein to be the driving force of all moving matter discussed in more detail in the section on ENERGY as a description of behavior when waves can drive behavior.

Compression waves, whether quantum size of electromagnet waves, do not create electrical current but rather they are electric current with no need of modification any further. Because waves are seen to wash over and through the brain, it is the same as saying that electrical current is passing through the medium comprising the brain. As both current and waves, the emission of waves in the vacuum passes the information along as current without further processing detectable by EEG equipment.

The CEREBRUM of the brain surrounds the internal structures of the brain like a cap with the top submerged in cerebrospinal fluid that submerges all of the parts of the brain and continues down the spinal cord. Along its surface is the gray matter of the CORTEX comprised of neurons packed very closely together with a very thick carpet of dendrites facing outwards, facing the flow of spinal fluid. Each neuron with its pack of dendrites emanating from the nerve cell body is an axon, the white matter, reaching into the interior of the brain with axon dendrites found next to a new layer of gray matter comprised as just described for the outer layer. More layers exist with gray matter, white matter of the axons and then more gray matter.

The layer after layer structure comprises the logic system divided into lobes of the brain that services the various needs of the body as set out herein in the section entitled ANATOMY. The outer layer of dendrites appear to be well to receive messages that need analyzing where the messages are waves washing over the carpet of dendrites. Each dendrite is well situated for capturing waves coming from various sources. These waves form the electrical current known to be essential to brain function.

Waves washing over the dendrites of the gray matter of the CORTEX must be captured and fed into the logic system that selects waves that closely match some criterion and passes them on into the interior for further processing. The logic result is finally sent to a proper part of the brain, all of which is discussed further herein in the section entitled NERVES and ANATOMY (of the brain), discussing where the waves are generated and the processes that take place.

The axons, the white matter, in the CORTEX are able to act as an electric circuit between the layers able to pass information in the form of electrical current to the next layer. The vacuum, discussed further in the section entitled VACUM, is a medium of particles so small that theorists treat it as though it doesn't exist due to its friction free construction and ability to form very reliable fields of gradient structures. Foremost of its list of capabilities is the ability to easily form virtually energy free waves or waves filled with substantial energy able to be the driving force of the particles of moving objects.

The most important of the abilities of the vacuum is the case made herein. Nothing in theory contradicts the mechanical theory of the atom set out herein able to perform the behavior of the theoretical atom, and much more. The models of the atom that can only perform a portion of the functions that atoms comprised of whole Hydrogen atoms gathered in the nucleus performing the known functions of the atoms. While the argument set out herein is that Hydrogen atoms were added to the nucleus, the same could be argued that protons were added to the nucleus and subsequently created their proton envelope and grabbed an electron. The end result is the same.

The elemental atoms in the neuron cells comprising the molecules are the same that have been discussed herein with the same properties. The principles underlying the gravitational field and the magnetic field are the same but for the confinement of the magnetic field in its envelope. Einstein's theories of relativity surely apply to both types of fields, not just gravity, in his general theory regarding a gravitational field. If the proton envelope captures an image by capturing the large peak particles of waves then by passing the image toward the proton nucleus, relativistic changes should take place involving perhaps infinite flattening enabling unlimited storage of memory.

The CORTEX structures of neural networks in performing the logic functions of the brain are essentially the same, with the numerous dendrites extending out from the body of the neuron cell, essentially covering or carpeting the outer surface of the several lobes of the brain and repeatedly passing them down to deeper gray matter structures would be an amazing reality of the brain. The numerous dendrites and connections between neurons are considered by some in search of a memory storage mechanism for the brain are underestimating the capacity of the brain if each of the many atoms that comprise the dendrites, the axon and the axon's dendrites are counted as efficient storage mechanisms.

Researchers may be busily seeking to discover from where all the brainwaves are being constructed but there is no doubt that they exist. The extended proton envelope is essentially an antenna like structure that could both gather and emit electrical waves. If any neuron cells are capable of emitting waves then any or all may have that capability since each carry the same DNA for the property. Even more so since they are each made of atoms.

Credible argument has been made herein that electrons in electrical circuits are not the current or potential that the circuit can possess but rather it is the vacuum and waves in the vacuum that are responsible. Theorists have seized on the electron as the only possibility since waves cannot exist in empty vacuum as they are supposed to presume. Therefore, any cell able to produce electric current can also produce unconfined waves for carrying information through any atmosphere.

No one can doubt the incredible capabilities of the

brain in its ability to retain and recall memories from a great many sources such that the mind and consciousness can be realized.   Theorists, biologists and biophysicists all deal in atoms to the extent that they are able to form molecules and cellular structures, hoping to be able to discover the secrets of the brain. The main argument here is that until the presumption of empty vacuum is abandoned, they may not be able to achieve success.   On the other hand, theorists are more likely to be creating incredibly long sets of equations that will describe these properties.

Each dendrite in the CORTEX of the CEREBUM and, even more so in the CEREBELUM must be able to capture waves containing entire images rather than just a signal pulse, and pass it down the dendrite itself for logic analysis with results of each passed down the axon to the next layer of gray matter, for logic analysis. The working capacity may be an actual or virtual infinite capacity if the mechanisms are contained in the atoms..

The nerve sensors of an afferent, or sensory, nerve is   able to capture the wave containing material and pass a copy along as current through the axon of the nerve to a specific destination. By the same token, efferent, or motor nerves may send the wave as electrical current through the central nervous system to cause muscle contraction or other adequate response. For all we know, the myelin sheath cells may be able to copy the material and amplify the messages.

Brain waves may have, as their source, specialized cells that process biochemicals capable of generating energy in the form of waves that can act as electrical current. These cells would be necessary for passing information among the parts of the brain but sensory cells collect information that exists in waves from the atmosphere to be passed into the appropriate parts of the brain for processing. Equally likely, each cell or each atom in each cell may be able to capture or emit waves with messages.

The brain is definitely the central processing structure of the body with various parts of the brain performing demonstrated functions that are more aptly described in the section on ANATOMY, meaning the anatomy of the brain. The point here is that in the brain, and all other objects are formed of atoms and molecules. It is the vacuum that we must understand as mechanical causative medium before understanding what is not seen as possible.

If a message is sent to all parts of the brain and each is able to determine if it must do something where others can tell if the message is not for it, then it would be architecture for a network. Another possible result could be that all parts of the body are sent the message and a logic system there must determine whether it is something it needs to do. The brain has evolved in complexity as the body has evolved in its complexity, clearly accounting for the size of our brains. It is not only the complexity of the body functions but the complexity of information that must be stored, causing the gray matter to evolve in response to both the intellectual and the body's needs.

It appears that the gray matter searches the memory against the inputs from the sensory systems to determine if the brain must take an action. In any event, the memory is searched in response to questions whether arising inside the brain, seen as intellectual questions. If the body need not respond, the input from the sensory system adds to the memory for future reference. This could be called opinion formation processing.

The issue being raised here is where in the brain are the memories stored and how they are searched. The functionality of the vacuum has not been analyzed by mainstream science, possibly due to a lack of means or equipment. More likely, it is because the vacuum is universally regarded as not having material due to the theoretical presumption of empty vacuum.

MEMORY, MIND AND CONSCIOUSNESS

Attempting to understand the mechanisms of the brain as properties of the vacuum is a far different approach of traditional theory. All that may be needed is for waves to be generated from sensory collectors and passed around to each of the lobes for analysis for services needed by the function they perform rather than the traditional pathways.

Protons exist in every atom where, most likely, are only those in the valence shell are able to create magnetic lines of force that are detectable as remote fields. A simple brain function would be to determine if a question must be answered or if factual information is being received. This would be the simplest of possibilities since we all know that the brain has much more capability than answering questions and storing factual material. There is ample information on the internet regarding the parts of the brain and the histology of each. Information about what bodily function needs to be serviced. In all the material that has been examined, there has been nothing about what functions the individual atoms of the brain may serve in terms being addressed here.

There may be various means for getting messages to the appropriate part of the brain or body. Virtually all surfaces of the lobes and structures of the brain are awash in or are close to cerebrospinal fluid surrounding the outer surfaces and throughout the brain leading into the spinal cord. Blood supply also reaches all areas of the brain as a possible medium for wave communication. Blood, spinal fluid and nerve fibers all meet at the base of the brain and leave as their separate material. Waves somehow reach the outer surfaces of the brain cap after entry below to reach the gray matter for analysis throughout the brain.

It may seem like a chaotic state unless each wave is identifiable as to source and possible need, a much different concept than usual where orderly hardwired paths are expected. An even simpler possibility would be to have every bit of information being stored in every possible place where waves cause a search within every database that is available, in valence shell proton envelopes.

Many of the   nerves in the brain interconnect to reach a region directly by means of neuron connections. Other connections to the rest of the body are through the brainstem and from there to the spinal cord. Waves that enter the spinal fluid must pass freely throughout the spinal fluid to reach perhaps the greatest amount of the body where the message is being broadcast.

The blood in the brain is precisely carried to every

cell of the brain to prevent any part of the brain from dying. The blood could be yet another means of spreading waves to every part of the brain though waves will characteristically travel much slower through blood but for the fact that the blood is moving in the direction that satisfies the need of saturating the brain with the information being received from the exterior by means of the sensory organs.

Theorists of brain activity would never conceive of the possibility that waves could be transmitted through the blood circulatory system.

Evolution is the designer of the body and the brain and every possible means for achieving efficient communication has likely been tried with unexpected results. Brainwaves must reach every part of the brain to determine if it should act after examining every wave for information it can use.

NERVES

The nerve cells of the body come in a variety of shapes and sizes depending on the function of a particular tissue. The main parts of the individual neuron are a long axon with many short dendrites growing out each end and a body generally at one end where the nuclear structure is found. There may be many insulating myelin cells growing around the axon up and down its length if the axon is outside of the brain. There are generally no myelin cells if the entire cell is within the brain. It is universally understood that within the axon is a low intensity electrical circuit that ends at the tips of the dendrites at each end of the axon.

The lower forms of animal life have ganglia that serve as a form of their brain and a memory system. Ganglia remain in the higher lifeforms to innervate the limbs and serving in other functions which may account for the ability to learn the fingering of musical instruments or automatic behaviors of the limbs by repetitive rehearsal under the supervision of certain parts of the brain sending out long axons ending with dendrites that innervate the muscles.

The section on BRAINWAVES emphasizes the role of waves in the transfer of information stored in the proton envelopes of permanent atoms of the brain. It may occur to the reader that the brain may not be necessary if all that is needed is in atoms having the needed information that is stored. The atoms in molecules may possess logic systems that are very specialized that are very old memories passed from generation to generation. Perhaps cell behavior now traced to DNA sequences could be held as vacuum memory called upon at various stages of cellular activity. DNA processes are able to correct errors but memories in cells are held in many cells that should be able to avoid errors.

Individual cells have behavioral properties, such as cell division, that is difficult to believe is directed by the DNA but the processes are repeated from generation to generation, even as a definition of a species. Spiders have a builtin knowledge of web structure that is quite complex in that there is instinctual knowledge that appears to be present. If this information is not in the DNA, it may be information that is stored in all the atoms of the cells where the repetition assures accuracy and permanence of atomic knowledge.

DARK MATTER MECHANICS

After a century of being assured by theorists and physics alike that the vacuum is empty space, it is difficult to face the possibility that theory and physics has been wrong all this time on the grounds that a material vacuum is mere clutter that needn't be of concern. The complete model of the universe was all this time a mere abstraction that the scientists thought would be too complex to be approached.

It may have taken cosmologists and astrophysicists to discover that the accounted matter of the universe falls far short of the amount of matter that fills the universe. Even so, cosmologists and astrophysicists are themselves theorists who are attempting to account for the matter in other ways before reaching the conclusion that it is contrary to their customary presumption that it is in the vacuum.

The structure of the tissues comprised of nerve cells is comprised of closely packed cells with dendrites at one surface and axons ending at another surface further into the brain body. A number of these layers, one over the other, satisfy the physical structures to function as the neural network logic now being mimicked in computer software.

Neural connections are generally a count of the dendrites which multiply the nerve cell counts by the average number of dendrites per cell. There are an enormous number of nerve cells meaning that there are an enormous number of connections that have a count that depends on the author publishing the figure since it is not possible to count one by one the connections so that the published number is an estimate or average at best.

A wave has electrical properties that originates at some distant source and reaches a sensory organ able to absorb the wave and distribute it perhaps throughout the brain as low voltage electrical impulses for storage in every atom of the brain. If this is so, it clearly outnumbers the dendrite count by infinity or even infinities of infinities without any cost in energy or space as a process that has operated in the universe since its beginning or perhaps before that in surrounding universes.

In other words, there may be very old memories stored in the proton envelopes of Hydrogen atoms but located under stacks and stacks of newer ones leaving the old ones to be unlikely accessed and if they were, they would likely not be intelligible. The proton with its magnetic envelope and its enclosed electron are perhaps the oldest objects of the space-time, as Einstein would characterize it.

DARK MATTER MECHANICS

The fact that the concept is being cited here is possibly some evidence of its existence, even though the concept may have been expressed elsewhere, which would strengthen the concept. We are able to build concepts out of other concepts but generally not completely from scratch. All the scientific and philosophical breakthroughs during the existence of the modern brain with all its logic networks, all may depend on some past experience or memory of an experience in the form of a collection of connected images. The neural network that exists most notably in the brain cap, the CEREBRUM, and the CEREBELLUM and other locations, is best known for selecting and identifying images, at least in computer implementations of neural networks. A set of images are submitted to the computer and a criterion and a best selection is made.

Biological systems are difficult, if not impossible, to implement on a computer due primarily to the extreme parallelism that is possible in a complete biological system. Even more difficult, if the physics or theoretical physics is not quite right, as when operating under the presumption of empty vacuum. While there are many dendrites along the surface of a cortex that encourages theorists to presume that is where memory resides. If computer implementations must be presented a set of images or data that the neural network is to make one or more selections in each level of the network, the set must be replaced to continue the process or start a new process.

The dendrites, safe to say, are constructed of biochemical structures comprised of the basic elemental atoms generally found in biological systems. Vacuum is the principal material by volume of atoms and pure vacuum may exist in the spaces between the atoms under current theoretical physics but explicitly devoid of matter. While the space within atoms is vacuum, as argued herein, it must be structured vacuum as a gradient envelope around the protons in the nucleus containing the electron. The gradient envelope must extend outward as the magnetic lines of force and the strength of the field is due to it being confined to an envelope. This would emulate a Hydrogen atom comprising the nucleus. The subject is treated more completely in ATOMS herein.

The line of force as an extension of the proton envelope is well situated to act as an antenna for capturing and emitting waves. If captured waves are sent down into the envelope into the vicinity of the proton and in the process is subjected to relativistic changes, such as fattening, to extremely conserve storage space as the proton is neared. A wave extracted and removed from the local atmospheric vacuum leaving the next wave to be analyzed by the next dendrite is unlikely. Saving data waves far exceeds the processes of computer emulations where reducing choices in each layer is the network algorithm of neural networks.

The forgoing mechanisms of atomic neural networks may not be even close to the reality actually occurring but the capacity of the brain for analysis would be beyond imagination but for the fact that we experience memory, mind and consciousness and analysis of our surroundings with such great detail that is beyond conceivability. Yet it does occur without much interference by our intent.

Theorists need only describe a behavior and reduce it to a mathematical analysis using a model to illustrate the mathematics, without any attempt to describe the underlying mechanisms. The behavior of the cortex structure is behavior like computer algorithms that emulate the neural networks of the cortex in logical selection against some criteria from a set presented to it. Theorists simply state that neurons have the ability to perform logic functions having capacity required due to the huge dendrite count. The forgoing seeks to present a mechanism that could be at work we each know exists.

MEMORY, MIND AND CONSCIOUSNESS

Other atoms in the dendrites active in the analysis could be infinitely greater than the best estimate of a cortex points of analysis. Dendrite are storing and popping information contained in a wave for analysis down the line. How many atoms in a single dendrite could be numerous allowing each wave to be analyzed infinitely many times.

A simple and admittedly incomplete logic could be as follows. An incomplete or confusing concept is treated as a question in the neural network for which it is fully capable of conducting a search until the question is resolved. A complete statement might simply be stored for further use perhaps in the conscious part of the mind but persistently in the back part of the mind until a fantasy or reality based resolution is reached. Because many atoms may contain an answer and many searches are performed in parallel, the question may persist until answered during a lifetime. If never answered, it may be regarded as a paradox or resolved as theorists have done, in quantum mechanics, as a paradox with many solutions being true.

Oxygen comes normally in the atmosphere as a bonded molecular pair. Two oxygen atoms carry sixteen protons in the outer valence shell, some of which is actively exposed to the outer atmosphere collecting information that can be passed into the body through inhalation. While we do not like being spied upon, these oxygen atoms could be collecting information from the atmosphere or from the body of people who inhale it.

In collections of people, it is not uncommon for belief systems to be regarded as factual in nature since it may be confirmed by all who are exposed. Belief systems are passed through the ages through writings but the original concepts are usually so outside of reason, they may have been the product of primitive slaves or captive animals, totally dependent on human caretakers who legitimately performed the role of gods. There is no reason for ideas to be based totally on human experiences, or even lower animal experiences, to not be passed from humans as inherent instincts.

Ordinary compression waves in the vacuum atmosphere, rather than photons, may be regarded as blasphemous to theorists who have lived by the empty vacuum presumption from school and all through their professional careers. However, it should not cause a fear of invalidating their theories since their concepts outlined here must satisfy the theoretical behaviors designed to precisely measure behaviors. It is their description that the mechanical models herein are designed to emulate. If theorists hope to prevent others from discovering or addressing mechanical causation then perhaps theorists should undertake the project themselves even if only as a purely scientific undertaking..

BRAINWAVES

The various parts of the brain are now discussed in terms of what they can do rather than what causes them to do what they do. The reading of brainwaves using electroencephalography (EEG) Is a way to measure brainwaves that are able to penetrate the bone, underlying layers of tissue and liquid of the head, and presumably able to wash over all the cells of the brain, virtually all at once or in sequence like a storm reaching the logic areas first and then the specialized brain structures.

Before discussing the how the brain processes waves, we must first discuss the nature of waves that are occurring as a constant basis that eventually reach the investigator using EEG technology for measuring frequencies in the customary form as electromagnetic waves, light. Quantum theory on energy is that all energy takes the form of quantum particles but these are not the waves that have been measured as accompanying moving particles of all sizes. The quantum waves cannot carry sufficient energy to move a particle of mass and either collections gather to move particles or there must be a different type of wave pushing particles of mass, argued herein to be the common compression wave with a gradient sufficient to capture and move larger particles.

Electromagnetic waves are like linked beads of quantum sized compression waves emitted by atoms having sufficient freedom of movement to spin while emitting the quantum size waves. Theorists characterize the quantum wave as photons because the presumed empty vacuum could not possibly be able to transmit actual waves. The larger waves that drive particles are not yet recognized as such since they can only exist in material vacuum.

Waves that exist in the vacuum containing molecular size particles, the atmospheres that theorists presume to be devoid of matter, other than the known particles, are the type that drives particles that must be of variable sizes due to the different sizes of particles needing to be pushed. Waves emitted from the proton's magnetic line of force acting as an antenna extending from the envelope can emit waves that may be broken into quantum particles, argued here as images that are being stored in the envelope.

Every atom that is a part of the biology has an outer shell that is incompletely filled where nonmetals are able to hold metal's electrons in bonds but nonmetals have several outer electrons able to be active in other endeavors such as gathering and holding waves from the environment while being firmly attached in a bond. Metals have exposed lower shell electrons that may be able to extend magnetic lines of force even though not able to participate in bonds.

Protein fibers are strings of atoms that can perform in wave collection and emission as chains of amino acids held together by peptide bonds. The behaviors being described here are certainly not a part of current theory because there is no description of behavior that occurs in vacuum. For that reason, the only argument that directly challenges conventional theory is to challenge the empty vacuum presumption and behavior that arises from that, nothing argued here arises from the material vacuum is not a challenge to any part of current theory.

Protons in the nuclei of atoms having a gravitational and magnetic field in the form of a gradient envelope is not counter to any of theory of physics or chemistry though the assertion that electrons are firmly held within the envelope is. The electron position is required to comply with quantum mechanics where energy waves promote electrons by moving them away from the nucleus. The density gradient of the proton envelope is changed affecting buoyancy and the position of the atomistic electron is able also to collect waves pursuant to theory.

Waves do not penetrate tissue but rather meet cellular tissue which absorbs energy and retransmits it in the form that tissue is only able, which is the form of electromagnetic waves. These are the waves that are being measured in the EEG experiments. The waves inside the brain cavity of the skull are waves in liquids which are waves that drive molecules and able to carry encoded whole images by atoms that have little freedom of movement. There is nothing preventing the quantum waves of electromagnetic waves to be collected and consolidated into whole images.

The brainwaves are not waves in the molecular atmosphere like sound, though some may be that may not be detectable, the existence of which scientists for the past century have refused to acknowledge, While molecules forming waves in the molecular atmosphere theoretically may not move more than their diameter in distance before striking their neighbor in mechanical theory, the molecules are not as packed in a gaseous atmosphere where we regularly are able to receive waves but the vacuum particles are closely packed directly adjacent requiring very little energy to initiate a wave of any size and may assist.

DARK MATTER MECHANICS

There is no theory about molecules in gases placing them close enough to push one against the other with any sizable probability but a wave in the vacuum containing the molecules are very reliably able to pass a wave as though they are in direct contact with each other. In the mechanical theory set out herein in VACUUM, a core of matter need only move less than the diameter, each radius, of the atomistic structures of adjacent particles.

The brain uses a substantial percentage of the energy of the body even though there is no known movement or muscle in the brain. It was just shown that there is very little energy used in creation of a wave in vacuum but that is precisely all that the brain does, is creates waves in the mediums that are available. Electricity is generated, by creating an intense magnetic gradient in the vacuum through which a closed circuit cuts through, in effect capturing the gradient density for storage as electric potential or current. The magnetic field that adds potential to the circuit is not electrons but rather the vacuum material in the form of waves. To again repeat, the movements of electrons are theoretically modeled as being current because vacuum waves are impossible in empty vacuum as presumed in theory. Just how waves are created and emitted from memory may have many possibilities such as using quantum entanglement to reconstitute compressed waves.

Quantum entanglement, argued herein in the section entitled ENTANGLEMENT, as channels of communication between once associated particles, established during progression from egg and sperm, is another means of communication not being treated to the greatest degree possible herein. There may be waves being passed but it is in the smallest of vacuum particles being passed as the boundary material of the envelope. These channels of communication may exist as an extensive dense network connecting all the atoms of the brain. The waves passed in this way are likely not the electrical current, though they may exist as undetectable waves. Science would have no way of detecting waves of this type, but will likely be able to replace gradient material removed in relativistic processes in storage of waves as memories.

No electrons are passed during generation of electricity even though scientists continue to refer to movement of electrons as electrical current. The vacuum gradient is passed into the circuit and it is waves of this vacuum that comprise the electrical current. Theorists are required to point to particles in passing momentum according to physics requiring theorists to assign electron movement as current for lack of any other particles in the theoretically empty vacuum of and around the atoms. For theorists, vacuum particles are an inconceivable reality and violation of theoretical norms, in view of the wholly fictitious empty vacuum presumption.

Energy is consumed by the brain and the existence of AdenosineTriPhosphate (ATP) molecules are extensive in nerve cell tissues that can be called upon to provide "energy" by breaking down to AdenosineDiPhosphate (ADP), with the loss of a phosphate molecule with its Oxygen bond. While other organic molecules produce energy, the ATP to ADP reaction is generally used to demonstrate the principle and as the primary source. Generally, a trigger mechanism causes the phosphate to break loose using enzymes emitting compressed vacuum, the "energy" of ATP stored when formed to be emitted when ADP is formed.

Molecules are physically tiny particles essentially comprised of the much smaller nuclei of atoms, and a great deal of space through which a vacuum wave can travel. Protons in the outer atomic shell are able to capture a copy of these waves and if in the third space of ATP, can emit a copy of the wave, according to mechanical theory used here where the atom is made of Hydrogen atoms with their magnetic envelope capable of holding information in the form of images. A trigger could be a very innocuous pulse that adds energy to the third ATP bond to cause it to break. The pulse could be a bit of pressure on the surface of a sensory neuron causing a much larger pulse that spreads throughout the sensory cell causing images to be emitted from the surfaces of the neuron that have recently been stored and possibly more from the immediate past.

It should be remembered that all cells of the body contain the same DNA as each of the others. Receptor cells in the retina of the eyes, for instance, are exposed to either one part of an image it transmits to the brain, or each receives an entire image which is transmitted to the brain, perhaps each with a different focal point but with the surroundings that can be analyzed as a single image, in thousands of locations in the brain, each superimposed on any or all of the past images stored on top of its stack. Images are then analyzed by the gray matter of the cortex.

Admittedly, the forgoing description of the retina could be in all detail the full picture of what happens, or at best, an abstraction of what might be occurring at the sensory cell. This description is not as abstract as theory which would be that the sensory cell is activated and sends an electrical signal to the next step, whether a ganglion in the spinal cord which passes a signal to the brain or directly to a brain lobe. During the theoretical account, no waves are generated, and yet, the brain is saturated with brainwaves of all wavelengths. Atoms along the surface of the neuron could be able to emit image waves unique to the cell.

Any processes that exist using the brainwaves are likely to be done virtually simultaneously, in parallel, performing their different functions. Just what the functionality of the waves are or what is their anatomy or the structure of their information, such as information being contained in the waves, are not a subject that is being reported upon other than, perhaps, in the most advanced research reports of cell function.

The different ranges of wavelengths could be the result of waves reaching into the brain through the sensory organs, perhaps some from some equivalent source that is not yet known. They are obviously concentrated from the form that they were received that allows them to be detected using the EEG equipment.

While the type of waves are not well reported, where the electromagnetic waves of linked photon particles, are generally thought to be the only wave that exists due to the empty vacuum presumption. They are possibly to be of the ordinary type, though light waves are likely to be tiny quantum compressions of vacuum, linked together in a sort of chain, as discussed herein.

The brainwaves occur in wavelengths in a range from a very low frequency rates from very low cycles per second to very high frequencies. They are divided into ranges from where each is thought to cause behavioral changes throughout the body according to their wavelengths. These are discussed in the literature in terms of their therapeutic ranges.

The infra-low and below are the slowest ranges and loudest or strongest of the brainwaves always be present and as though having a timing function much like the clocks in computer science. For computers, the beginning of each wave marks a point that signals some functions to execute and the end of the wave marks another function either to begin or end an execution. Whatever exists between the beginning and the end is generally unspecified but with brainwaves, there could be a great deal of information.

The brain waves are divided into the ranges in the literature that are each addressed as affecting moods and mental states or other behaviors within the body. Therapies based on brainwaves exist that professionals use with professional proficiency in the control of professional associations.

Training is achievable in reaching levels in each of the segments by various means and by professionals in the field though some have argued with some evidence that the states may be placebo effects, a position that is vigorously challenged by those practicing the art. The states and associations are associated with the ranges are described at https://brainworksneurotherapy.com/what-are-brainwaves where the states and training to achieve the states are described.

Theorists and physicists alike have concluded that light is linked photon particles and that electricity is movement of electrons in the spaces between the atoms of a circuit in which a potential exists. There is a presumption in both these sciences that the vacuum is empty space leaving no alternative but to presume that electricity and light are being generated in a way to affect movement of particles since there are theoretically no alternative but to presume otherwise. If one is allowed to presume that the vacuum is a material medium, it is a prime candidate for being ordinary compression waves in the medium that is the vacuum for both light and electricity.

The thesis being argued herein is that such not

only is the case, but that the unaccounted matter in the universe is the matter comprising the vacuum. Brain scientists seeking to discover the source for the brainwaves, that undoubtedly exist as moving particles, are compelled by the empty vacuum presumption to discover a biological source that can contribute either electrons or photons in formation of the brainwaves .

All that is needed is to discover electricity in the insulated nerve fibers that end with exposure of the conducting material that allows release of the waves in the circuitry where they are known to be electricity to become brainwaves in the surrounding atmosphere of the brain. At the synapse between nerve cells, there is a release of not only chemicals but of electricity and it is well known that in such an event, waves are generated that is generally detected as static, that interferes with receivers designed to emit or read intelligible waves but will be interpreted as unintelligible static that tells us of unprocessed electricity released into the atmosphere. The static is most likely the result of inability to interpret the content that the waves may be holding.

To us, brainwaves are unintelligible waves that are being released by where the atmosphere is being exposed to unprocessed electricity leaking where a break in the insulation of a circuitry exists. We know that it is a collection of the various wavelengths that are the brainwaves and by mathematical means, using Fourier analysis, they can each be isolated to become what is known as QEEG or qualitative electroencephalogram analysis. Technology uses a carrier wave that contains other wavelengths used in broadcasting. It appears that the wavelengths designate regions of the brain to be affected by the waves.

The nature of the particles that must be present in the vacuum to function as it must, an infinite variety of particles comprise the vacuum in which waves may exist, many of which may not yet be detectable by scientific means but may be read by unknown means in the brain. The process of all the messages in modern networks where all information is broadcast to everyone in the network containing the address of the node which each is supposed to read. When the address is finally reached, the delimited message is finally read, stored or acted upon.

All atoms have an active outer shell of valence slots in which chemical activity can take place. The current theoretical model of the atom depicts electrons orbiting around the nucleus while seeking to interact with photon quantities of energy in the form of electromagnetic waves in the atmosphere, each of which will promote the electron to a new more energetic orbital. This is in essence according to the quantum mechanical model that controls the theoretical process argued here to be satisfied by electrons moving to a new level in the proton envelope as waves are absorbed.

The electromagnetic waves that promoted the electron in orbit are then emitted as a new wave of a set of photons, quantum units of energy, emitted while the electron is in orbit to cause the familiar sinusoidal wave structure drawn in space, allowing the electron to return to its former orbital. If each promotion of the electron is counted as a bit of information, the energy that is stored as new orbitals is lost to history. The process is likely mimicked by nuclear proton envelope emissions, causing the atom to spin while emitting the new wave or waves are emitted from the line of force acting as an antenna.

Theories guide research and the orbiting electron model was first introduced with convincing argument relating orbital energy and electrons with no argument regarding possible mechanisms. The model has remained a fixture of theory without challenge other than the quantum mechanics to prevent the electron from a nuclear crash. The theory is that electron velocities prevent change in orbital diameter using curved space to prevent change without injection of energy, all in empty vacuum. That basic model has been augmented by quantum mechanics but has never been challenged on what should seem to be obvious grounds. Electrons in orbit are the only means for wave creation in theory and so are the brainwaves.

Brainwaves are described as electrical impulses but the nature of the waves is not generally discussed, perhaps due to the unknown nature of waves. If EEG equipment are thought to only read wavelengths of electromagnet waves so that information, if any, is crammed into quantum bits having internal structure, a very possible reality is infinite particle sizes of vacuum as argued herein.

Theorists describe electrical current as electrons being pulled away from the atoms and forced to flow as current in a circuit under electrical potential. This concept is an accommodation necessitated by the presumption of empty vacuum calling for a particle that can be attributed with the movement of electrical current, argued here to be movement of vacuum.

A better presumption is that the vacuum is a material medium capable of transmitting energy by means of ordinary compression waves and in the case of electrical current; it is the particles of vacuum in the form of compression wave peaks that is the current in electrical circuits. This means that the nervous system that carries information about the body through neurons as electrical current need to accept compression waves from the sensors that collect information from various sources to be interpreted by the brain.

Visual images are captured by the eyes by the spread of dendrites extending from the outermost ganglion layer of the of the retina that capture electromagnetic waves as electrical potential pulses that are sent through the optic nerve to several regions in the thalamus, hypothalamus and midbrain where they are fed into the memory systems, a process that is discussed in detail in the chapter under the title ANATOMY. Numerous other sensory receptors are located throughout the body that essentially behave in the same way but using various mechanisms for creating electrical signals and transporting them through extensions of the neuron cells as electrical potential to the appropriate regions of the brain for storage as memory.

The physiology of the many more sensory neurons that receive information other than the five senses, some exist in the organs, the muscles and anywhere else that pain or other sensations may be felt have sensory neurons placed throughout. They function by accepting waves of electricity that pass through the dendrites and the axons of the neurons and perhaps up the spinal cord to reach the appropriate part of the brain where they are felt as pain or pressure, as the case may be, as a compression wave peak emanating from the organ must contain identifying information.

Because the vacuum is ubiquitous everywhere, in the atoms and between the atoms, all that need be done to have an electrical wave of current to begin its journey through the brain is for a wave passing through the outer or inner atmosphere reaching a receptor. The receptors all are equipped with nerve fibers that pass the wave to a part of the brain that be interprets the wave as information that may need immediate attention by passing the wave over internal receptors connected to the various parts of the body through nerve fibers passing down the spinal cord.

The forgoing is common knowledge about the functions of the brain but there are mysteries regarding brainwaves and their function. Other realized structures in the brain are the logic system in the gray matter of the brain forming neural networks able to interpret received sensations by comparing immediate information with past memory and recognizing contradictory and incomplete information as a question requiring past memory to be dredged up to complete the information using past memory in the neural networks.

A number of different methods for understanding the different parts and structures of the brain have yielded a great many sound results and understanding. However, like all the other sciences based on theoretical physics, physics or mathematics, the focus of attention is on behavior and behavior control without regard for mechanisms or using cause and effect analysis.

Virtually all the brain is devoted to sensing and body control based on sensing organs using such terms as electrical or pulse communication. Current thought on electrical transmission is electrons leaving their atomic structures under potential pressures but without chemical effect on the atoms losing their electrons. Vacuum movement would have no effect on chemical structures.

When it is realized that the vacuum is filled with matter where core particles are surrounded by gravitational and magnetic gradients with no empty space, wave and electric transmission is interactions through contact passing the momentum of core particles from one to the next. The transmission of a wave structure involves a very slight movement of core particles from one neighboring particle to the next in a dense but fluid vacuum ultimately transmitting the momentum into memory of proton envelopes for immediate use or for posterity.

Electricity is moving density packets exactly like the waves in the surrounding atmosphere. While we see tightly packed cells submerged in spinal fluid or blood, in reality the nerve cells, spinal fluid and blood are vast expanses of vacuum particles separating tiny proton particles causing very little or no obstruction for passage of compression waves. When structure and variation is added to compression waves, a rather complex mechanical behavior must be taking place.

From the point of view of the vacuum, the molecules comprised of atoms, comprised of connected protons of Hydrogen atoms, the structures the brain are describing a very complex scaffolding in which vacuum particles have complete freedom in which to carry out the business of finding and reconstructing a three dimensional replication of the surroundings. Those stored on the very top of the memory stack could form a basis for recognizing each electrical signal that is in the form of a free unconfined wave.

MEMORY, MIND AND CONSCIOUSNESS

In the same way that mathematics is constructed of carefully thought out logic using numbers, carefully thought out descriptions in the vacuum comprised of an infinite collection of particle sizes in creating a machine where the mechanisms for transfer of memory and theoretical energy able to move the body parts through muscular innervations. The brain, regarded in this way, is a complex device using common means over and over again can be understood.

While the forgoing may be very difficult to imagine, try imagining every atom maintaining a three dimensional internal scaffolding of quantum entanglement channels able to pass information, images and whatever else the sensing system has carefully put away for future reenactment for our pleasure or needs. We may realize two channels for the information we need. One that sends signals faster than light and another much slower than light where the former allows time to react to the latter.

Functions of the mind must all be taking place in parallel by accessing all the recent memories being held in all the atoms, possible only in the outer valence shells of the atoms, with immediate reenactment of the present. We may be living in the visions of the future in view of the faster then the speed of light passage of the information traveling through the small particle quantum web of entangled communication channels.

Scientists and theorists have informed us that what we imagine about our future is in reality a logic system that is able to predict the future based on remembrances of the past. We live in our inertial frames of large particles both in the atoms and in the vacuum in and around the atoms but quantum entanglement are passing information it sees that is in our future relative to our perceived present experiences.

When a need for sudden movement or even ordinary movement is perceived to be needed, the entangled channel may have passed information about its past that arrives a short time interval in the future of our present danger or need for movement based on our ability to see into the future. Preparation for energy stored in molecules perhaps may need to prepare for the needed movement allowing us to move out of the way of danger based on our ability to perceive the future in real time and not based on a search of the past for similar events that tell us with some probability what is about to happen. There is in fact a real possibility that we actually see into the future based on discoveries in experimental physics of quantum entanglement rather than on some analysis of possibilities.

MEMORY, MIND AND CONSCIOUSNESS

One might argue that we do not receive information from the outside world that is in the future but the vacuum is made of particles that were once associated with each other in the bowels of a star that exploded causing them to be separated. This could create entanglements between all the particles of reality since we live in an infinite space and possibly space time according to Einstein. Science does not quite understand quantum entanglement but only in the context of information between formerly associated particles. This implies a communication channel capable of transporting it at super fast speeds, an inexplicable process in view of the presumed empty space where structures are impossible to be found.

Activity of the brain may take advantage of a reality that we know very little about due to our stubborn adherence to the empty vacuum presumption. Very little about reality is in fact the product of randomness or probability though science must think and derive theories using these form of calculating behavior due to lack of information about reality perhaps only due to lack of studies about the vacuum.

The description herein of quantum entanglement is based on current experimental findings though without any discussion of mechanisms that may cause the behavior being witnessed in the experiments. Einstein, by examining the data, calculated the findings in his theories of relativity perhaps without any thought to causation. Particles growing in size due to acceleration were fundamental in many of his calculations together with findings regarding the speed of light and its observed changes in certain environments.

Einstein's theories have proved very mysterious without the ability to understand his mathematics, the language he used in describing reality with great precision. He viewed all of reality as a set of mathematical equations but was unable to unify them all into a single one. Equations need no explanation regarding causation and he persisted on the presumption of empty vacuum as a theory though admitted in a speech, only one time, that it must be a material substance, but not like that of the aether theory.

In the segment herein entitled ENTANGLEMENT, the speed of light and its relationship to inertial frames, used by Einstein in his equations, a discussion on the mechanisms has been set out to extend his theories using a means that he refused to address, the mechanisms as the basis for what the equations revealed to him that must exist in the vacuum differences from on inertial frame to the next. He established that light can travel at different velocities in one inertial frame relative to another especially after being accelerated, where light travels slower.

In the discussion set out in the section herein entitled VACUUM, the particles of the vacuum to allow the known behavior of friction free movement, must be well lubricated with ever smaller particles contained in structures and surrounding structures. Entanglement allows information in the form of waves to travel in a channel, or inertial frame, formed of smaller than usual particles due to stretching of envelopes causing smaller particles to comprise the channel.

There is what has been referred to herein as a ubiquitous sea of continuous smallest particles of the vacuum around all particles in and around all the various structures that exist in the vacuum in the section entitled ENTANGLEMENT that was not discussed perhaps in great enough detail. While it must be present to provide the lubrication for friction free behavior, it might also be available for travel of waves that cannot be detected using instruments of observation outside of its inertial frame due to being ubiquitous. That does not eliminate its presence or its use by biological entities such as super fast communication within the brain.

DARK MATTER MECHANICS

Entanglement creates a channel of communication between once associated particles but the ubiquitous sea is an environment in which waves can saturate the brain with information before neuronal channels can provide or the brainwaves can provide. In other words, we may be living in the future, if ever so slightly, ahead of what our sensory mechanisms can provide. We know in advance what happens if we move in a direction because we see it in advance happening, even in the outside environments perceiving waves in the ubiquitous sea of tiniest particles.

The information that is passed as electrical pulses are not likely, by means held in modern theory, as release of electrons into the spaces of nerve fibers, rather as discussed herein as waves in the vacuum. Creation of electrical pulses of information takes some time to create as a compression wave and to transmit it through ordinary vacuum takes ordinary time while the same information could have been already transmitted by other means in preparation for the real time information to arrive.

There need be chemical reactions in creation of electrical waves. For the process to begin and finish its purpose in the material vacuum perhaps augmented by hydration of ATP producing ADP and an energetic wave. Signals received from the sensing organs are weak and augmentation is a means of spreading the signals and data.

ATOMS

It may seem strange to discuss the elemental atoms in the context of memory, mind and consciousness but, in the context of dark matter mechanics, the atoms are the fundamental building blocks of all the biological species in which we are a part. In fact, we are perhaps at the end of the evolutionary chain of biological species but that does not mean we are therefore above all that took place before us in every way or that activity in the evolutionary process is not continuing.

Our species, in the animal kingdom, like all the others in the animal kingdom, begins with the egg that is then fertilized and if all goes well, the embryonic progression begins. But before all that, it is the atom and then the molecules that start it all off and the study of the atoms then may seem to make sense to discover what part they may play in our development and evolution.

When speaking of atoms, we are speaking of elemental atoms because all biological species, and most other objects of significance to the topic here being addressed, are at the lowest level of understanding constructed of atoms, other than their particles, to the extent of our knowledge.

The elements are the objects of the Periodic Table of the Elements where they are listed in sequence according to the number of protons, the atomic number, are in the nuclei and, in the rows, electrons in the outer valence shell are able to participate in molecular or chemical bonding.

The atoms are far too small to directly observe in any great detail but we know their characteristic outputs and can observe their clusters taking the form of molecules, which even then may not be directly observable. The result of not being observable, their construction is largely theoretically based on their energy outputs and effects on their outputs based on their inputs where theoretically, the protons are clumped together in the nucleus while the electrons find their way into orbits which change when they accept light energy whereupon they emit light according to their orbital.

The atoms are made of protons and an equal number of electrons as though each atom is built by the addition of Hydrogen atoms bound together by a strong nuclear bond at their protons leaving them to remain in their active states until the valence shell is filled and then the row is covered by a new valence shell in the nucleus where in the periodic tables, a new shell is formed that is listed as a new row. This all occurs during creation of the atom as a permanent structure, while the table compares one atom to the next.

The chemistry of the atom is determined by the outer shell, the valence shell, where the beginning is at the left of the new row in the periodic table. The valence shell has as many slots as the row in the table depicts where the first row has two, the second and third have eight, and each column under these elements have similar construction in the outer valence shell. Most tables are color coded by entry showing the elements in the columns on the left of the table to be metals and those to the right of the table to be nonmetals, except for the final column.

As the valence shell slots are filled with few remaining empty slots, those atoms in those columns are the nonmetals with their outer valence shell filled but for a few in the right end of rows and their columns of the Table. Once the outer valence shell is filled, the filled atom is an inactive noble gas. An atom with one more proton has the beginning of a new valence row. There are exceptions to the rule that are listed separately or in the middle of the rows where their atomic number is listed in the table. Metals are generally able to form bonds by filling the empty slots of a nonmetal.

The significance of all of the forgoing is that the current model of the atom illustrates the electrons in orbit while it is being argued here that the proton and electron are an inseparable unit of the atom where the electron is held in the gradient field of the proton, the envelope, and waves are encountered, they are able to penetrate the proton envelope and cause the electron to move further away from the proton and the proton envelope is allowed to extend as the magnetic line of force, extending as far as the magnetic field can be detected.

In current theory, the electron orbit is increased in diameter as new waves are encountered, which can be detected in the new electromagnetic wavelength emitted by the electron. Therefore, a new state of the atom is remembered only as long as the wave has not been emitted as a new wave, a very short while.

If the atom is built with active Hydrogen atoms in the nucleus, the electron obeys the quantum mechanical model with the electron increasing its distance from its proton as waves are add to the waves being stored in the envelope causing a change in the density structure. An electron is promoted until the density structure returns by processing new waves. A new wave is then emitted causing the atom as a whole to spin, emitting the sinusoidal electromagnetic wave made theoretically of photons but more likely made of relatively small, quantum valued, compression wave. However, compared to infinity, discussed herein under INFINIATY, quantum waves may be very large but small compared to waves that drive particles to movement.

In the brain, thanks to electroencephalography (EEG) experiments, as waves reach a sensing apparatus, the entire brain seems to light up as electrical waves wash over the brain. What the purpose or function of these waves are thought to be is an indication of the activity of those portions of the brain that the waves reach. They could have another deeper function if only the mechanisms of the brain may be better understood.

In the section herein on ENERGY, there is some evidence that the theoretical energy in the presumed empty vacuum is addressed as a substance able to cause movement of mass, the same function can be caused in presumed material vacuum by compression waves much like ordinary waves in any medium where the molecules are pushed together to form compression peaks leaving behind the troughs where the core particles move apart.

Furthermore, the most familiar form of energy is captured by passing a current carrying circuit through an enhanced magnetic field, the proton envelopes, that are pressurized by means of coiled wire around a metal, or magnet or empty space, create a pressurized vacuum in the envelope, under electrical potential, is passed into the current carrying circuit as current instead of the theoretical electron used as current.

Waves of energy coming from all directions can form a complete image that enters the proton envelope. In other words, compression waves in the atmosphere are converted to compression waves in the nervous system as electricity where waves are stored, perhaps as described herein. The model for a memory system is completed as memory is stored in the vacuum of proton envelopes.

If a Hydrogen atom in the outer shell of the nucleus captures a wave that penetrates the proton envelope with its momentum, the wave may be captured and stored for posterity, perhaps after being processed using the means described in Einstein's theories of relativity, described further in the section on

MEMORY and on RECALL.

The atoms are created in stars fusing hydrogen protons one after the other until a final construction of an atom is completed, perhaps with the first Hydrogen that may move to another region where no more are added. Theorists say that free Hydrogen is captured by stars where ever larger atoms are created and the largest of which formed when the star collapses revealing a dwarf star that was there from the first formation of the star or, according to theorists, is created by the collapse of the star.

Theorists seem to hold firm with the theory that the dwarf star is created during the collapse but argued here that it is there before the star is formed as a means for its formation. Its presence is probably causing the high pressure and heat of the star but could also aid in the creation of proton particles out of the material vacuum.

If the particles of the atoms are created near a dwarf star core of the star that is hidden after the star begins to form and revealed only after the star blows away the material surrounding the core. Protons could first be formed somewhere near the dwarf core and immediately the magnetic gradient envelope begins to collect around the proton that buoyantly moves the proton to a new level within the star were other protons with their gradient fields reside to begin to be bound together to form the larger atoms. There may be even older atoms formed in a universe surrounding ours.

Theorists responsible for the big bang theory are unable to predict what was involved during the big bang but are able to describe the event moments afterward. It could therefore be imagined that it occurred in a much older universe since the material vacuum was already present that allows the physics we know today to exist where waves of energy are formed as compression waves causing our universe to be created, as argued herein. The differences between theory and mechanics for the big bang are discussed in detail in the first volume of this series. The inflation of our universe could be vacuum rushing in from the older surrounding universe.

Atoms and their role in storage of memory is discussed further in the section entitled BRAIN as closely packed waves near the proton core of the envelope. If that is the case, there may be very much older atoms than any formed during the creation of our universe, complete with proton envelopes with its electron. Atoms are being created in stars in the universe, but there may be atoms that contain very little information that can be drawn on in the formation of thoughts and memories using them. There has been virtually no effort to describe mechanisms of memory so far where focus is on the effects or behavior of memory.

We tend to think that we only know what we learn during our lifetime but there are concepts that are not being learned based on memory alone. Science is not easily convinced that some thoughts alone have any scientific value unless supported by experiments or direct observation. For theoretical physics, there can be nothing accepted unless supported by correct mathematical proofs presented along with a model that illustrates the mathematics. For mechanical theory being applied in this series, the mathematics has been done since mechanisms are being sought here, largely, to support theory.

The vast abilities of the brain are difficult to understand such that some have suggested that thoughts are acquired from an outside intelligence. Our atoms may have existed in failed civilizations due to the end of their planet or that did exist on our planet for which we have no evidence. A person, or many people, may have accessed memories that are very old and told their stories but it would have to be a fictional account since the teller would not be able to know where the memory came from.

MEMORY, MIND AND CONSCIOUSNESS

Today, current memories are passed from parent to child and then from teacher to student, and so on. It is commonly thought that our knowledge is the total of what we learn during our lifetimes from our experiences. It may be that none of that can be understood by our minds without some of the old memories, at least the complexity of nuances that are realized. The common quoted question of whether we are born with a clean slate, the answer may be no, if memory is a property of physics.

If this is the case, the most recent memories are stronger and memories that are repeated the most as well. Any that are ancient most likely will make little sense and would be covered up. The ones like the meaning of shapes or those of arithmetic where logic is a part may allow us to make since of what we learn now or make learning easier. Invention is sudden insight of something that has never been experienced by anyone could be an ancient memory rising somehow to the top.

As described here, memories behave as a first in last out stack that may be arranged logically along with parts that allow the date and time when learned. We are certainly not at the mercy of physics when it comes to memory which must be understood as a mechanism, an aspect of reality that theory does not address. The approach used here is therefore not theoretical physics at all because that is a science belonging to mathematical theory applied to discoveries in physics.

There may be mechanisms that operate in the atoms that cannot be anticipated by merely adding particles to the vacuum in such a way that maintains the properties that are known to exist. There are particles being called atomistic vacuum particles that are core particles of matter surrounded by a gravity and possibly a magnetic gradient of very much smaller size particles ranging from largest to the smallest at the boundary. From this description, a very much smaller yet set of particles must exist comprising the atomistic structures around the perimeter of the gradient particles.

Quantum entanglement gives another set of particles that have been anticipated in the gradient structure of the proton envelope involving associated particles with a group gradient envelope that when separated will stretch that to an extent that the small boundary particles will occupy the entire envelope as very small particles, being, in effect, a changed inertial frame. These particles are so small that they possess very little energy of inertia or momentum allowing waves to pass very quickly, experimentally found to be faster than the speed of light. Researchers remark that information is received about the associated particle before changes in that particle occur, in its future.

Vacuum particles are so small that physicists have been allowed to presume that they do not exist even in the face of facts that obviously reveal their presence, such as the presence fields that affect behavior in the presumed empty vacuum. Gradient particles and their gradient particles reveal that particles in vacuum must have a range of small to very small, a proven infinity in the section on INFINITTY.

For all these particles, there must be yet a smaller or smallest particle in an inertial frame or possibly in the universe in which all particles are awash, a ubiquitous sea of smallest particles. In this medium, waves may also be generated that cannot possibly be of any use to us in our search for reality but for the brain, in which miracles seem to be happening, it could be making use of that medium to pass information around at speeds that put entangled channels to shame. These waves would not be in channels but rather would be without bounds able to inform parts of the brain what to expect in the far future, perhaps.

Mechanisms that exist below our ability to directly or indirectly examine have been mathematically described in terms of probabilities, largely thanks to

Einstein who was not interested in speculating on mechanisms that cause behavior. His focus on behavior was a trait that theorists have adopted to this day while not being required in any way to describe causes for the effects as behavior.

We are able to anticipate into the future and even into the far future generally thought to be by relying on past experience. If we see visions of the future, they are generally disregarded when there is nothing in the past to support them. So long as we have free choice, a vision of the future, whether based on physics or past experience, can be changed, perhaps, unless the path to the future is such that it demands the outcome of the vision MEMORY

T   here seems to be no good model in theory and brain science for storage of memory in the brain or in the rest of the body where it also must exist. The favorite description of memory in the brain is of the very many dendrites that connect neurons, certainly enough to retain all the memory that one could amass during a lifetime. Along with this assurance is the established trace of memory recall that experimental evidence supports where stimulation in different parts of the brain can force conscious patients to recall different memories depending on where the stimulation takes place. The explanation is that a trace or path of memory is created with new memories that can be retraced whenever recall is activated.

Computer science has stepped into the fray with regard to the logic systems of the brain citing the gray matter structures presenting the structures of a logic network commonly called in computer science a neural network. This network has been modeled in software and possibly in hardware allowing many possibilities to be presented to the network with a query requiring the best choice be returned of the many choices. Layers of these networks can be implemented where the first layer will narrow down the choices and from that returned list, a better set or, in the final layer, best choice is returned.

Computer science also teaches that nature of data storage in terms of pointers to a set of instructions or as a collection of raw data, but in either case, the data is a set of bits in the form of bytes or words. If the sought after data is an image, especially a color image, it is more than a set of on and off bits that form the image but is more complex. Images are stored in many different formats and the first few bytes of an image is a structure with slots for the name of the format that was used in storing the image, generally the size of the file and other data needed to read the image.

A television camera may be a good replica of the visual system of the eye where photons or quantum sized waves enter through a lens that focuses an image onto the retina at the back of the eyeball where nerve receptors collect the waves and pass them through a nerve trunk of many neurons into the visual system parts of the brain. From there, apparently the visual stimuli are analyzed through the logic system for meaning and from there passed to the relevant parts of the brain where action is required. If a bodily response is required, a wave is sent through the brainstem to the spinal cord where electrical stimulation is read and an appropriate action is hopefully taken of muscles that need be activated. The action is then sent to the brain to confirm the required behavior.

Depending on how memories are stored, if a great deal of the brain is used for storage, only a small part of the brain is used for logic and body behavior. If there is a very economical means for memory storage, then most of the brain is likely used for nuances and fine body movement is processed in the brain. This is known to be the case in humans where fine movements of many parts of the body are under control of the brain.

MEMORY, MIND AND CONSCIOUSNESS

Brain science indicates that information from sensory organs cause massive amounts of brainwaves to wash through the brain, perhaps for every part of the brain to receive information and to choose for themselves if it is relevant to its function and possibly for storage wherever the waves are accepted. In that case, the logic system is like a thinking mechanism rather than a first action center where new information is passed through the logic system but only soon after, or even much later, the information is passed through the logic system to meet its purposes.

The brain has a memory system that is active during consciousness that is alert to current stimuli either within the brain as thoughts or arriving from outside the brain and first passed through the gray matter, the dendrites of nerve cells and through the white matter comprised long axons to the next layer of gray matter and so on and finally reaching the THALAMUS to select an appropriate interpretation. Brainwaves are emitted that wash across the outer regions of the brain where more logic and interpretation occurs and appropriate parts of the brain bring forth appropriate memories for use in creating thought. The mind is the entire body sending and receiving waves of information including all the parts of the brain that call forth recent and recently used past memories.

DARK MATTER MECHANICS

To the extent possible, all the functions of the brain are accessed simultaneously in parallel continuously throughout waking hours producing information waves called brainwaves that are passed over the CEREBRUM, or brain cap, covering the internal parts of the brain and is comprised of the CORTEX or outer layers of the CEREBRUM washing across it from front to back over the various regions of gray matter and into the THALAMUS with functions that might well be called the brain functions, parsing and distributing information to and from the CORTEX and the BRAIN STEM and spinal cord.

The forgoing is a rough analogy of current thought regarding the operations of the brain where the parts of the brain and the behavior and stimuli they excite have been discovered but the only mechanisms that are known are the electrical stimuli passing through the neurons and chemicals exchanged at the synapse connections of the neurons. Because all the sciences honor the empty vacuum presumption of theory, the description that follows is what may or must be occurring that adds functionality to the brain using the dark matter vacuum. It is therefore thought that the electric current passing through neurons is vacuum waves and more likely in complex biochemical reactions.

MEMORY, MIND AND CONSCIOUSNESS

The waves in the vacuum are compression waves having various structures and in the brain, it is argued here that the waves can represent images that the brain can easily and quickly pass about, store, copy, modify, retrieve and interpret which leaves very little else for the brain to do. It is a closed system having many responsibilities to the living organism of allowing a useful understanding of the outer and inner surroundings of the body together, causing useful responses generally passed down through the generations.

To the extent that memory mechanisms have been addressed by the various scientific fields engaged in brain function, the connections of neurons or cell behavior is the current favorite due to the vast number of cells and connections being made. Another is creation of molecules that represent memory that are perhaps passed around through the blood system or through the axons of neurons to the various parts of the brain and body.

This treatise is devoted to understanding the role of the vacuum in brain function, a prospect that is inconceivable for today's scientists due to the presumption of empty vacuum. The behavior and useful properties of the vacuum are examined using the mechanisms of the atom where most of the properties of vacuum are located. What may seem to be an inordinate amount of attention being paid to the atom herein is for a reason, with certain modifications to the atom of supplying a reservoir for storage, the functionality and properties of the atom are maintained as discussed here and elsewhere herein.

In the section entitled INFINITY herein, it should be noted that an infinite selection of particle sizes must be necessary for the vacuum to maintain its known properties of allowing objects to pass through it free of friction, without there being any empty space whatsoever to maintain consistent behavior and retain and maintain structures such as fields, waves and channels of communication established experimentally to exist that are likely used in brain functionality.

The proton is known to have a magnetic field or envelope able to affect the behavior of objects that pass in and out of it. The magnetic field is described herein as an organized gradient of larger vacuum particles nearer the center core proton of matter and gradually smaller particles approaching the outer boundary. The surrounding boundary of the proton envelope is comprised of very small vacuum particles that prevent larger particles from wondering in and out of the envelope. Each of the vacuum particles are referred to herein as atomistic particles having a surrounding gradient field of their own. It is in the proton envelopes that likely storage spaces for information may reside, in the vacuum.

There are several locations or lobes of the CEREBRUM that are active in memory activities as determined using scientific methods such as electroencephalography (EEG) readings of locations of brain activity where memory is being accessed. Also, using awake patients to respond to direct stimulation causing a set of memories to be brought to the forefront of the mind of the patient is no indication of where the memories are located, whether there is a specific central location or decentralized locations.

In the section herein entitled VACUUM, the vacuum is described as either empty space according to theorists or as material made of matter such as possibly the dark matter discovered to be present in the universe but with no specific location. If the matter of the vacuum is present, there is little likelihood that, even though very likely to be comprised of particles, science may never be able to isolate the particles of the material vacuum because they are likely far too small and varied to be individually detected, especially if it is an essential part of the mechanisms involved in the search for particles.

DARK MATTER MECHANICS

The vacuum and its relationship with the atom is likely most important in understanding brain behavior and ability if memory is stored as impressions of images or remembered activity stored in the vacuum. For that reason, some understanding should be gathered regarding the atoms that comprise every part of the brain. As a general statement, it is possible that every memory could be stored in every atom of the brain subject to being recalled to be used as the memory that we are all familiar. If that is the case, then the capacity of the brain is unlimited. However, memory and recall serve different functions of the brain depending on where and how the atoms are situated.

Many chemical reactions take place in water where the reactants are molecules that are larger than the water molecules. In these reactions, whether commercial or as in experiments, the water is disregarded in the search for the new and expected reaction results, even though the water may play an essential role in the reaction that is taking place that requires the procedures to be undertaken in water. This is becoming more and more apparent to chemists and now, many times the chemical properties of water are being indicated in chemical equations perhaps as an intermediate reaction.

The same may be said for the vacuum where

forces that take place in the vacuum are attributed to masses and their projected fields that obviously take place in the vacuum. The same can be said for the brainwaves that are passed around the brain when all we really know of them is their wavelengths that contain smaller waves within a given wave that can be mathematically extracted using Fourier analysis. The waves electric current of a sort and need not be converted but only need be placed in a circuit to directly convey the information we are unable to detect in the infinitely small particles of the vacuum in which the waves are generated.

The structure of the atoms are set out herein as comprised of Hydrogen atoms in the nuclei having more than one proton and it is their electrons that are described as behaving in the periodic table of the elements where they are described using the orbiting electron model of the atom and the orbits are described as existing in shells represented by the row of the table. The electrons are contained in the proton envelope or in the proton magnetic lines of force that extends out into the surrounding atmosphere, to the extent that they can be measured. The magnetic lines of force are likely able to collect waves from all directions to be passed down into the envelope of the proton core. These waves may undergo relativistic changes and well understood real changes, such as particles gaining matter and being flattened similar to actually being accelerated, according to Einstein.

Possibly, the waves can be stored within the body of the proton envelope after being compressed, perhaps by ejecting part of the particles and removed through emission of a new wave. These new waves are understood to be caused by electrons in orbit causing the sinusoidal shape of their structures but the same effect would be caused if ejection of the wave particles, or quantum sized compression waves, were to cause the atom to effectively putting the electrons in a temporary orbit while remaining in the proton envelope spin or the wave uses the line of force as an antenna for the same effect. The emission of new waves should put the electrons in closer proximity to the proton effectively meeting the requirements of quantum mechanics and the new reduced energy orbital.

If the electron is instrumental in emission of waves after being exposed to the energy of incoming waves, the incoming waves would naturally cause changes inside the envelope causing the electron to rise within the envelope in accordance with quantum mechanics of the atoms where orbits are known to change, to increase or decrease by quantum amounts according to theory and wave emissions.

MEMORY, MIND AND CONSCIOUSNESS

It can be seen that allowing the nucleus of an atom to be comprised of active Hydrogen atoms in shells depicted in the periodic table of the elements but where an electron in a conventional orbit, a wave will cause the electron to move into a new orbital and remember the event until a new wave is them emitted, erasing all memory of the event. While the inner shells of the atom are also Hydrogen atoms, or even simply protons with their magnetic envelopes. Their chemical activities are suppressed by shells that overlay and prevent their activity while the outer shell is allowed to remain chemically active as the valence shell.

Another little problem can arise in theoretical behavior of the atoms and waves. The electron is essentially bound to live inside the proton envelope. While its location can change, even change drastically, it likely remains attached to its proton by an entangled channel.

For other reasons, just as the photon is likely to be a compression wave that is identified as a particle for theoretical reasons, electrical current that is theoretically identified as movement of electrons is more likely movement of compression waves, misidentified for the same reason that photons are likely to be quantum compression waves. In that case, the brainwaves that are identified as electrical waves in and outside of the brain cavity can easily pass into the neuron as electrical current without any modification or processing and emitted as waves outside the brain for the same reason, as brainwaves.

If current is coursing down a neuron that abruptly ends, the current may continue to the next neuron without any processing or into the tissues of the brain that are not neuronal. This is likely in a dark matter vacuum even though molecules have been detected that are associated with the passage of information from one neuron to the next at a synapse. These molecules and tissues may have information or not. There may be any number of functions attributable to the synaptic conveyance of material.

Einstein described many changes that occur during acceleration in his Special Theory of Relativity that were also apparent in changing gravity conditions described in his General Theory of Relativity, on grounds that gravity is the same as, or in fact is, acceleration. Changes in mass were an experimental discovery that plays a significant part in the two theories set out by Einstein. If gravity is a gradient as being described herein, then the same changes must be occurring in a magnetic gradient, only more quickly and with more intensity. It is those properties that are likely happening to waves that the atoms are able to collect and rather than being subsequently emitted though a new wave must be formed and emitted that identifies the atom.

As core particles become more massive by entering into an increasing gravity state, they will buoyantly be separated from the smaller particles of their gradient fields, a process that likely continues leaving the fine grained gradient material behind and the larger particles to continue on toward the proton particle while suffering length contraction, flattening or vice versa. These waves may form an image of each initial wave which will be stored within the proton envelope, one wave structure after another as images, making a sequential record of the images that are continuously captured, even if the waves are quantum elements of electromagnetic waves.

This is a credible account for the memory record that is being kept that allows us to reach back in time to recall events that are the memorized images stored in proton envelopes. Of course, a single proton envelope will be a weak source of memory but each proton in the brain may be able to store memory without increasing the volume of the brain, especially if the vacuum is an infinite assortment of particles where an infinite number of which will remain infinitely negligible in volume. Memory storage is useless unless there is a credible means of recalling memories being stored, a topic that discussed in the section RECALL herein.

It should be noted that each atom in the brain was in the past closely associated with every other atom throughout the body, originally in the egg and sperm, and as the body grew in size, the atoms may have retained a means of communication in the form of quantum entanglement. Every molecule has an envelope that when entangled, a joint envelope containing molecular atoms also exists holding each in relation to the other. Entanglement is the joint envelope that remains after separation but in a stretched form causing only boundary particles to remain.

When the joint envelope is stretched, it becomes a tube comprised of the tiniest particles in the vacuum as the outer boundary becomes more prevalent in the tube forming in effect an inertial frame far different from the surrounding atmosphere forming a communications channel between atoms or collections of atoms as bodies. Waves passed through an entanglement will not only be extremely fast but will be a unique communication between the previously associated bodies, perhaps able to reconstitute the stored changed waves due to relativistic effects.

MEMORY, MIND AND CONSCIOUSNESS

While quantum entanglement may be one way for communication to be maintained, there may well be other means for retrieval of memories. The electron is another gradient field that may act in the same way as the protons in storing information. The mind is able to retrieve memory and also to copy it and break it apart into pieces that will have the ability to recall what never happened as stored, perhaps in dreams or in simple thought states which themselves can be stored and recalled.

Remembering that we live in an infinite universe, it may be possible for an infinite amount of memories be stored that is sequential, temporally stored allowing the mind to maintain communication of the memory data according to the time it was first stored or other logical means however the logic system decides. New memories must also be able to be stored according to the time so the mind may recall perhaps an older memory. There must be allowed a very efficient means of restoring a set of recalled information.

The grey matter of the brain is comprised of nerve cells that can sprout dendrite tentacles in formation of what is known as a neuron logic network able to read a mass of data and choose an image according to a set of criteria. Many such logic layers can be used to refine and create a range of data that is reduced in each layer until a final selection is made and the CEREBRUM and CEREBELLUM are CORTEX structures that have several of the layers necessary to make choices among many sets of stored data.

Computer programs that mimic the logic or neural network accepts an original collection of images that is swapped out for another collection from which a final selection may be made. How the mind replaces data that is captured to be processed may involve the process of quantum entanglement, able to view information from any of an infinite number of atoms that store information. Whatever the process is, it is both magical and efficient.

While the forgoing description of information storage and retrieval as the memory process we all possess, without having a vivid memory of how it may work, reading information that would be stored as images of the past may require an intricate neural network that resides in the grey matter of the brain. The forgoing should allow science to rethink other attempts to understand memory processes of the mind, perhaps aided by cellular or chemical means.

Theorists use fields to describe the strengths of force acting on an object at a given location relative to sources of the field. Faraday's magnetic lines of force, as Faraday's tubes, were reinterpreted as mathematical fields describing the collection Faraday tubes acting together as density values. The sources of these tubes were never investigated with the presumption of empty vacuum. These forces must be an extension of the individual magnetic forces that surround the protons and the equality of electrons to protons must also be respected. The lack of a viable theoretical means of storage, and of course, the section on RECALL of memories cannot be acceptable.

The current theoretical orbiting electron model of the atom is based on energy exchanges and the role of electrons in electricity as current, necessitated by failure of any other particle for that purpose. How the atoms fit into reality is not a feature of the theory. How orbiting electrons are able to form bonds in chemical reactions has always been inexplicable feature of the orbiting electron model. The same for the theory that orbits around both chemical reactants is the means remains inexplicable.

This section discusses the atom in great detail at variance with theory. Vacuum material has been ignored in theory where the essence of theoretical physics is to understand the behavior of new discoveries without attention to the causation. Physics itself has not isolated the particles that comprise the vacuum because of the size of the largest, let alone the smallest, is beyond being isolated, earning vacuum the description of being truly dark matter.

Had cosmologists and astrophysicists not discovered the shortage of matter in the universe, matter in the vacuum would still be in evidence by the behavior it exhibits. The fields are certainly not created by the mathematics that occurs in the empty space and the endless supply of wave material would eventually have to be explained for a complete understanding of reality.

One day there will be recognition of matter in the vacuum that would necessarily need to be understood by biophysicists searching for how memories are stored and retrieved in biological systems. Counting the connections and dendrites of neurons could be sufficient to store something of significance perhaps to store nuance to the motions the body is capable requiring a logic system and connections throughout the body of nerves that sense and those that react to stimulus. Someone must analyze the mechanisms of dendrite memory because theorists are not tasked to discover mechanisms, or believe in them.

Electrical waves sent through the spinal cord to the

muscles of the body may contain more than just a brief shock stimulus causing a response. Ganglia exist within the spinal cord that are capable of decoding any information contained in the electrical waves sent from other sensory organs of the body, such as the brain or including the skin. These waves may also contain information about the urgency, and so on, that induced the wave, read at the level of the ganglia in the spinal cord. Of course, internal messages are passed about within the brain where perhaps decisions about further action takes place.

Using the massive number neurons and their extensions fails to explain how they might be used in memory formation but there is no mechanism in the literature but only the number of neurons and dendrites that may be deemed possibly sufficient to retain memory for a short period but not in such detail and for a lifetime. Memory storage in the vacuum of proton envelopes should be unlimited in amount and duration. The brain has the capacity to make copies and to cut and paste in very creative ways involving storage and retrieval of old memories.

The concept of storage of memory in the vacuum has not been suggested in the sciences due solely to the presumption of empty vacuum. The old aether theory had the matter in vacuum standing still with no other function but acting as luminiferous aether conducting light waves. It is unfortunate that theory is not supposed to dig deeper than behavior. Much of very early discoveries about nature were at a time when attribution to a deity was mandated at risk of incarceration or death. Surely we are past that.

As the atom is now modeled as a collection of protons bound together in the nucleus in numbers equal to the atomic number set out in the periodic table of elements and equal number of electrons to protons in the neutral state. Better, all the chemical properties of the atoms depend on the outer valence shell of Hydrogen atoms in the nucleus, or the electrons according to current theory as set out herein in great detail.

The section on RECALL describes the possibilities for extracting memory from the proton envelope, make copies and cut and paste the memories as stored with little engineering complexity. Proton envelopes containing the magnetic gradient could accommodate electrons within the gradient such that memory could be stored in the electron envelope for transport and emission. Theory offers little in the way of storage and even emission beyond the processing of immediately received light. Theory has the electron change its orbit due to accepting new waves as is stated in quantum jumps to higher energy orbits. The connection between the electron and the proton envelope avoids the possibility for storage of memory in any amount over a single wave for duration beyond the next wave emission.

Current theory, as with all theories, goes no further than behavior, and therefore depicts the electrons absorbing the energy of an electromagnet wave and in turn emitting a new electromagnetic wave but how it is done is not discussed in theory. Consistent with theoretical physics, no mechanism that could cause these events is set out in the currently modeled theory other than labeling the waves as photons so that theoretical models are only abstractions. See the section herein on ABSTRACTION that omits what is deemed immaterial or facts not on point, most notable is the role that the vacuum obviously performs in reality. Of course, there is no law requiring scientists discover or report all they know.

The section on ANATOMY discusses the anatomy of the brain and the functionality. The LIMBIC system of the brain is used for processing memory comprising (1) the PREFRONTAL CORTEX, (2) the HIPPOCAMPUS of the TEMPORAL LOBE and (3) CEREBELLUM relaying information to the BASAL GANGLIA. (1) is responsible for short term memory able to hold around seven items for a short term. (2) Holds memorized information in unlimited amount and for an unlimited duration. (3) Skills memory such as typing, playing a musical instrument or playing computer games is processed in the cerebellum and relayed to the basal ganglia.

Brain studies using the electroencephalogram, the EEG, read electrical signals originating from within the brain. The process is used to detect brain waves that reveal certain states of the brain used in research and therapy that are thought to reveal based on the named wavelength ranges rather than wave content. The waves and the resulting behavior of a subject can be described but the waves themselves are only known to have wavelengths and amplitudes. Much more may be learned but only if presumptions are correct. Waves are now described as strings of photons and electrical current is moving electrons, both are being challenged herein.

In physics, all particles of mass must possess a magnetic or gravitational field, or both, and these fields are being described herein as gradients capable of causing the behaviors in field theory.   It is well established that waves, particularly electromagnet waves, carry with them momentum. A wave travels as the particles of the vacuum become compressed as the cores are forced together in the early stages of the wave peak formation to carry the momentum of the collection in the peak. As particles entering the wave peak, the cores are pushed together while their gradient fields are pushed aside allowing the cores to behave as a particle with momentum. When the peak is formed of particles next to a magnetic envelope of a proton, it penetrates the envelope causing the envelope to inflate.

Theory suggests that quantum waves are photon particles. To be fair, a wave could exist in a medium and enter free flight at the beginning of empty vacuum. The wave peak is launched, so to speak, into free flight as a photon without a core particle or rest mass. But such an entity could not occupy the same space without disruption and a wave is a spherical entity and seen as particles during extraction. The end of material vacuum may be the edge of the electron field but still does not stand up to scrutiny.

The atoms, being argued here, are somewhat different than the theoretical model. Electrons must be held in the proton envelope or field while protons are attached to each other in the nucleus. The shells described in the periodic table of the elements are protons in the nucleus arranged in shells rather than electrons alone in their orbits. The quantum mechanical model is satisfied when a photon of energy strikes and penetrates the envelope wall causing the material within the envelope to inflate causing the electron to buoyantly rise or float a short distance away from the proton, promoting the electron into a higher position away from the proton through buoyancy. One possibility is wave emission causing spin and the sinusoidal shape, reasonable when matter is being fired out into the vacuum.

The electron is also an atomistic particle with its own magnetic field constructed much like that of the proton as a magnetic envelope. As an energy wave penetrates the proton envelope it must affect the electron envelope, with its limited size, causing it to emit a wave of its own. This could cause the atom as a whole to rotate or spin while emitting quantum waves to create a new electromagnet wave where the body of the Hydrogen, the proton envelope, is the resource from which the wave material is drawn. Waves using force lines is another theory herein.

Put in the simplest form possible, a better model of the atom and quantum mechanics can be constructed if the vacuum is acknowledged for what it is. The photons are waves in a vacuum filled with atomistic particles and some waves come in the form of information in the structure of the wave, as images. If images are collected by the extended proton envelope and stored near the proton core in a compressed form by perhaps losing some of the gradient material, the process of collecting waves and then emitting a new wave from a reservoir of wave material would be complete, deflating the envelope after being inflated by capture of the wave.

Capture of a wave will naturally cause a change in the material structure of the gradient within the envelope causing the electron to jump buoyantly to a new level as depicted in theory as the quantum jump. Furthermore, a wave emission forms a sinusoidal shape theoretically due to the electron emitting its wave while in orbit or the atom begins to spin. We know that atoms spin while emitting a wave because electromagnet waves have a sinusoidal geometric shape formed as the emitter moves in a circle but if emitted from an envelope extension, no spin is needed.

The current theoretical model of the orbiting electrons perhaps allows quanta of energy to be stored in increased energy of orbitals of electrons. Analysis of how the model would function is simply not possible since it was not constructed originally to function but merely to happen. A particle must gain velocity to reach a higher orbit but proposing electrons to hold photons of an entire electromagnet wave is not conceivable. Theory does not specify the trigger that initiates a new wave more importantly; theory does not specify what holds the electron in orbit since the meaning of energy is simply motion, defined as motion or acceleration of mass.

Theorists propose that the only memory retained in the atom is temporarily stored in the energy of the orbitals that changes as a new wave is accepted or emitted. The orbitals are not observed directly but are presumed by the change in wavelength as they are being emitted. Theorists are not required to explain the mechanisms of behavior of a model or even if mechanically possible. A photon attaching itself to an orbiting electron will cause the orbit to decrease but for the momentum of the photon, but momentum is a directed energy which could either cause the orbit to increase, decrease or to wobble, depending on the directions of the electron and the photon. The difficulty in expressing all that could be why so much is left out of the model and theory. An abstraction need not explain how the behavior works, but it should know that it exists.

Theoretical mechanisms of emission are also not made clear in theory but when emitting a quantum of energy, a balance of momentum like recoil of a rifle, will push the electron away from the direction of the emitted photon, either back into a lower or higher orbit as loss of energy or gain of energy. By the same analysis, the capture of a photon by an orbiting electron will push the electron away from the direction of the photon. Relativistic changes will also occur as a wave or electron changes its velocity. A particle gets smaller as it is slowed down and furthermore, a particle will carry waves which must be at least two waves, one that overcame inertia and the other being momentum. These will be transferred upon contact to the electron to achieve the theoretical effects, once the presumption of empty vacuum is lifted.

Over the last century, due to Albert Einstein, the orbits follow probability paths that form what is known as the electron cloud where it can be known with a certain probability where an electron might be found. The original mathematics for calculations of electron orbits was taken from the astronomers whose calculations for the orbits of planets were generally used. A more modern method for calculating electron orbits comes from wave calculations where wavelengths are calculated using characteristic wave functions, too complicated to be discussed here.

Discovery of the nucleus was achieved using Alpha particles fired through a metal foil where it was discovered that a hard or solid core prevented passage of the particles through the center core of the metal atoms being bounced back in the direction that it came. The Alpha particles were seen to be deflected with greater intensity nearest the nuclear core and less so with distance from the core as though like charges of bar magnets of the nuclear core and the Alpha particles in a magnetic field of a bar magnet. The Alpha particles were deflected away from the core as though the core and particles were charges of like poles of a bar magnet. Gradients in the vacuum may be the basis of the bar magnet but the poles cannot be isolated.

There are other ideas about the electrons such as being contained in various balloon shaped structures with each belonging to an electron coming from computer modeling techniques representing electron clouds that do not interfere with each other. These shapes are probability clouds and the newer wave function is regarded as a wave packet as being described here for moving particles of all sizes but the electron in orbit can only be found using the wave function that describes the probability of its location. The atoms are not observable so that all the models of the atom are made up from detectable emissions.

The orbital model was devised after the nucleus was discovered and the magnetic field theory for suspended electrons was based on the behavior of Alpha particles that miss the nucleus. If the electron is held within the proton envelope at a certain height above its proton, it may in a sense be in orbit above its proton and therefore be difficult to locate other than by a probability function and if the atom has spin, even more so.

The quantum mechanical view of the atom is that the electron accepts and emits waves perhaps when it has reached some amount of capacity whereupon, the waves it emits will be the exact same size, the quantum or photon, but sequentially as it is in orbit around the nucleus. In empty vacuum, where there can be no other, the quantum sized wave would be emitted by the electron envelope which certainly limits the size of the wave.

If a larger size particle is detected, not seen, then there is no other conclusion to be reached but that it is the electron. If the proton envelope itself emits a wave, perhaps as a single ordinary compression wave as when a stream or current under pressure is induced in its environment, that emission would naturally be seen as an electron. The quantum sized waves may contain visual information while the larger might contain a sound image, perhaps.

DARK MATTER MECHANICS

The original behavior of the electrons in orbits was no doubt patterned after the planets in orbit and they are not observed to emit, other than from a central star. However, the orbiting model solves other visible behaviors such as the canon ball problem interacting with gravity but the mathematics of orbiting bodies is frequently tested today in outer space. In all such tests, there is no reason to link orbiting bodies with memory or with intellect.

Philosophers might be thinking that perhaps the mind exists outside the brain or body for the reason that the extent of resources are so vast that it seems impossible for the brain to be able to access its extent. On the other hand, It is easy to believe that our intellect is developed strictly through biological observations and logic using the blank slate model of memory at birth though spiders know a great deal about how to build a web without being schooled.

It may seem that atoms with information could account for supernatural events such as ghosts, demonic possession or cultism by recognizing the reality of material comprising the vacuum either in the mind or atmosphere. The concept itself should not change reality and as for the mind, the presence of sudden possession of the mind is not likely since brainwaves must be present having a function and

147

most likely to saturate the brain with information but the evidence must rest in external studies by the experts using a different presumption regarding the vacuum.

The content of the brain may be inherited to some extent but it certainly can be augmented by newer or older matter, as written material from some time in the past. One might decide to read material that may be categorized as harmful by influencing behavior or beliefs in contrast to material that might be categorized as beneficial to society. Obviously, the solution is not to remove material that may be read but we, or some, know how memory works even though not the mechanisms and bad books must be augmented by good instruction.

There are vast resources from which we learn and are influencing us but there was a time before we can know the mental capacity of early man. Early man may have had the mental power as the present mind, other than the things they left behind for archaeologists and sociologists to find that appear primitive, perhaps due to the lack of outside resources. There is no real way to know the capabilities of the mind until means for recording and publication of their intimate thoughts, opinions and observations become available. We can only measure variations among our own species which cannot reveal the mechanisms involved other than when injuries reveal lose of some particular capacity.

RECALL

Recollection of memories and possible means for reading memories by biological systems, we know exists. It may be physical processes that may be more appropriately discussed as natural processes described in physics and theoretical physics if as waves that have been collected and stored deep in the magnetic gradients. It may be very primitive processes present in primitive biological lifeforms and readily retrieved in natural temporal sequences, if the vacuum is in fact a material medium. Current theory must admit that the mind and sensory organs generate waves of electrical current that is obviously stored somewhere and can be readily retrieved as memory of the past in such a way that it can be modified to form imaginative variations of the past.

As with all the processes that are described anywhere herein that are functions of the vacuum are generally original and not described elsewhere due to the presumption of the empty vacuum where there are no functions directly attributed to the vacuum where no functionality can occur in the presumed empty space. We know that processes occur and must have a means to occur.

All particles in the universe possess at least gravitational fields that are argued herein to be gradient structures, called atomistic structures taking the form of larger atomistic vacuum particles gather near a core and gradually smaller particles occupy regions as the outer boundary is approached. This structure is argued herein to be able to attract and repel other atomistic particles relative to the core using principles of buoyancy.

The structures that are magnetic structures are also gradient structures but contained in an envelope bounded by the smallest particles in the region. The magnetic structure is a steeper gradient but having a limited distance that is unlike the gravitational field. There is an intraparticle ubiquitous sea of smallest atomistic particles filling the space between the outer boundaries of the atomistic particles in a medium holding all the particles together and forming an infinitely effective lubrication system and a means of communication between gradient structures that are within other structures at least within a frame but possibly within the universe.

MEMORY, MIND AND CONSCIOUSNESS

Memory and the ability to recall past events and images that were witnessed in the past is recorded as a natural process that we all experience privately with proof that our fellow humans also experience through their expressions and constant display of the same abilities. Storage in cells such as neurons or their dendrites or biochemical structures have each been thoroughly researched with no convincing results. What has not been even discussed as a possibility is storage of memory somewhere within the vacuum, most likely directly due to the presumption of empty vacuum.

The means of storage is discussed in the ATOMS section herein and some suggestion of how memory is retrieved for use in the brain, mind or consciousness. That discussion generally came down to memory storage taking place as images, as waves collected from various regions, outside or inside the body or brain. It is proposed there that the images are relativistically compressed one after another in order by time perhaps in special atoms or in special locations but more likely in as many atoms as the waves can reach automatically and as a natural mechanical means.

Atoms are generally very old, created in the stars where they are finished as permanent structures with the ability to gather waves as images even outside of the biological environment as an infinite capacity for storage. But, there is no indication that these images are ever released by any mechanism until they are incorporated into a biological environment in the form of mental images that are used as memories of the past without the ability to erase them.

Storage may be a straightforward process of the properties of a material vacuum that has not been discussed heretofore in the sciences due to the empty vacuum presumption since all the processes here described are arrived at through known processes of molecules and atoms such as the magnetic field as a gradient and the boundary of magnetic fields referred to herein as the proton envelope that limits the distance it can exist and lines of force as an extension of the envelope defining the magnetic field of the magnetic proton atoms.

The lines of force may function as the existence of antenna for both gathering waves but also for emitting waves extracted from memory. Emitting waves by the electron within the body of the envelope serves perhaps a different function such as for relieving pressures from absorbed wave material as quantum strings of waves in electromagnetic wave structures, a more automatic function controlled by the amount of waves absorbed such as relatively bright light for which a response as relief by emitting it, as we know happens.

Einstein's inertial frames are regions in which the mathematical parameters differ under his general theory of relatively specifically in regard to clocks running slower in denser gravity or gravity wells. The theory is based on the fact that gravity is a measure of acceleration and the same effects that are created in an accelerated inertial frame where it was established that accelerated particles gain in mass. The mass gain is a measurable fact while flattening is due to length contraction in the direction of acceleration.

A corollary where energy is equal to mass times acceleration or mass times velocity squared, the mathematically equivalent to acceleration. If our mechanical theory that motion is caused by driving waves using the vacuum particles in line of the motion, moving in increased gravity where the vacuum particles are larger and more massive, the wave itself causes measurable increases in mass even while there is length contraction according to Einstein' special theory, most likely just a measurement problem and not physical as here needed.

There is a presumption that there is no matter in

the vacuum as being presumed herein which leaves only behavioral observations described in mathematical form as inexplicable behavior. We need not guess what the thinkers at the time of Einstein's equations regarding causation was since the aether theory was in full bloom at the time and the theorists attempting to attribute causation using aether were preempted by Einstein's rejection of causation.

While the aether was thought to be a standing gas, there was nothing regarding the particle sizes of the aether as being addressed here. A gradient could be regarded as a standing gas where it is only the gradient sizes that cause movement in it where a particle will move in the direction of particles its size. It might be pointed out that large particles have larger gradient structures and the smaller particles nearest the perimeter are actually denser and will exert greater force against a larger particle. Whether meeting the envelope directly or its extension, as Faraday's line of force.

The atoms and their gradient structures have a dense perimeter of very small particles than wave peak's larger particles, due to compression, can only be penetrated by their momentum, the particles nearest the edge being pushed by their neighbor behind will gain the momentum necessary for entry.

MEMORY, MIND AND CONSCIOUSNESS

Throughout the discussion regarding waves, there is an assumption that a different kind of wave than that of light is driving particles in motion and is being generated by sensory organs. That need not be the case when closely analyzed. Information stored in computers are in page sized segments even though continuous from one page to the next. Additionally, we must assume that EEG readings are of the ordinary waves, electromagnetic waves having quantum sized segments. These should be readable comparable to the page sizes, one quantum wave after another.

How information is stored in the envelope must have a relationship with how it is extracted as memory recall. It must be reconstituted and passed out as a wave to be interpreted by the logic system. The memory is stored in the envelope near the proton as a stack of memory that is compressed where the most current is at the top and older memories are to be found at some depth, perhaps measured as some distance in time. The best place to store the memory as data in the dendrites of the CORTEX to allow a continuous amount of data to be available for logic analysis.

The entire surfaces of both the CORTEX regions of the CEREBRUM and the CEREBELLUM are both floating in the subarachnoid space filled with

156

cerebrospinal fluid and also the internal surfaces are filled in the lateral ventricles including the BRAINSTEM and from there drains into the central canal of the spinal cord.

Most of the sensory organs feed their input to or near the surface of the CORTEX at a specific location for each of the organs. The current models or hypothesis attribute types of the sense for each organ but certainly the lobes that have been tested to serve the type of sense is trained to react according to experience or excite regions with an electrical charge or chemical emission. There is no correlation with brainwave emission or the meanings of these.

The sensory organs and their regions of the brain are regarded as transducer organs. The afferent nerve is the sensory receptor nerve and the efferent nerve innervates muscles or receptor organs and both lead to the same region of the spinal cord. The conventional categories of receptors follow though some believe there are from 21 to 32 sensing abilities and excess ones are not listed.

Chemoreceptors of the olfactory system dealing with smell, taste buds lead to the GUSTATORY CORTEX, aortic bodies able to detect changes in oxygen.

The nerves lead to the OLFACTORY CORTEX.

Photoreceptors include cones that detect color in three types or wavelengths, rods detect intensity or dim light. Ganglia cells reside in the retina and the adrenal medulla.   of the eyes lead to the VISUAL CORTEX in the OCCIPITAL LOBE.

The AUDITORY CORTEX is located in the TEMPORAL LOBE of the CEBRUM.

Menchanoreceptors respond sensing from the skin to touch as pressure or distortion that includes form, roughness, stretch, slip, vibration receptors nerves lead to the parietal lobe as the primary SOMATOSENSORY CORTEX is a narrow region just behind the FRONTAL LOBE.

Thermoreceptors perceive either temperature above or below body temperature with a receptor for each. These lead to the SOMATOSENSORY CORTEX.

Nociceptors perceive pain related to heat, cold, excess pressures or mechanical deformation and chemicals. These lead to the SOMATOSENSORY CORTEX.

There are numerous references, some in greater detail, on the internet and the forgoing appeared to be relevant to paths for wave to take. For each of the forgoing systems for managing the senses, each seem to have their own cortex structures for logic systems but none of these sensory receptors act on their own and none are reported to be related to the brainwaves. For purposes of the subject being discussed here using the vacuum to communicate waves injected into the cerebrospinal fluid is able to reach all surfaces of the CEREBRUM and the CEREBELLUM to allow the entire body to know of all the senses detected.

If each of the cortex regions mentioned have a memory system as well as a logic system, perhaps broadcasting the most recent memories into the cerebrospinal fluid will reach all receptors will be reached, but the mechanisms for recall requires an understanding of the systems.

The proton envelope should be regarded as an inertial frame of its own that is quite different than that in which the sciences take measurements and must be understood as compared to behavior outside of the proton envelope. An image wave obtained through the line of force leading from the envelope will be largely stripped of their gradient by being compressed into the peak of the wave which is allowed into the envelope. Without their gradients, the near core particles will be very dense and easily sent down into the proton region while even gaining mass as they fall while suffering contraction or flattening and the vacuum will have little small particles available to form a gradient.

Recall of memories are likely a reverse process where if the smallest of particles can be injected into the regions where memories are being stored, then perhaps the dense infinitesimally stored waves may be reconstructed by infusion of the tiniest particles available and the reverse relativistic events may be allowed to take place through injection from entangled channels discussed in the section on ENTANGLEMENT. The more recent stored waves will be reconstructed then will lift the wave toward the line of force acting as an antenna and be released into the CORTEX for analysis in view of new sensory detection.

The movement now in brain science is to treat it as a computer program where none of our computers have the means for making choices based on a holistic basis as being argued here. Scientists are seeking hardwired connections with perhaps a logic CORTEX system for making choices for what nerve should be sent a pulse back to enervate a correct muscle set. By alerting all the regions of the logic system for the entire brain will allow all the systems to determine the strength identification of the sensation as it affects other regions.

Current theory leaves muscle responses to the ganglia structures in the spinal cord and the same cerebrospinal fluid is available to broadcast the condition using image waves, the simplicity of which will allow all the logic systems to understand.

Waves created within a quantum entangled tubule created as a result of past association with the particles, the protons in this case, are waves of particles that are the smallest or smaller than any in the surrounding atmosphere. Infusion of these types of particles could cause an infused gradient giving the wave buoyancy that could force stored particles to migrate upward and be as if hydrated to their former states as the largest particles in the surrounding atmosphere and perhaps the entire sequence driven out of the envelope and stored again in the same or another proton envelope as a process of recalling a sequence for possible processing.

The proton envelopes involved might be found

anywhere or everywhere within the complex of brain tissues and release structures that may be identified and passed around by any of a number of means where they are passed through perhaps the logic network of the grey matter of the brain.

While there may not be an eye or ear in the brain that can see or hear the images, the images received from the eyes and ears are not well understood regarding how they are processed in the brain as images, the same processes may be able to read the images produced from the memory system if only as echoes from the past or however memory is perceived in individuals. It is likely that they are passed through the logic network as the target allowing current images to remind us of something in the past.

The ability to store and retrieve entire sequences as a single object would introduce an efficiency in the memory system whereas the orbiting electron model of the atoms can store bits of information that may add up to a color but in any case, the bits must be stored and constructed into an image or sequence of images too complex to be very readily understood. If the brain must put these bits together in a full image and find a place to store it where it can be later retrieved, the brain would have to be fully developed before any memory could take place in the evolutionary process.

If the atoms are instrumental in the storage as described herein, the memory process would be fully in place early in the evolutionary process, perhaps guiding the brain in its divisions and motor functions. But, if that is the case, then memory may be in perhaps biological entities where it would not be expected. Early single cell organisms may possess a fully developed memory system along with bodies that are suited for their existence. When the genes of many plants are examined, we find they have much of the same genes as the mammals and even ourselves meaning that they may have memory capabilities while lacking the means for physically expressing them.

Memory alone does not mean that thoughts can exist without many of the brain structures that exist for processing them. There is the logic system that allows past events to be coordinated with new images that are entering the brain structure. The massive brain size of the human is largely to serve the muscle system and the many other duties that requires supervision and be responsive to the many capabilities of the body which is discussed in the section on ANATOMY.

ANATOMY

The brain receives information from the surroundings and interprets it and then either acts on it or simply remembers it. There is very little understanding or consensus of where and how memory is stored and retrieved or how it is processed in the structures of the brain. The purpose of this thesis is to seek an understanding of the processes with the understanding that a medium must exist that has been totally ignored with properties that hold promise for expanding our knowledge and understanding using a mechanical theory of vacuum understanding of reality.

The brain is covered over the top with the CORTEX tissues in folds and regions between folds and obvious lobes and the following terms may help in reading material regarding the brain. Gyri (p) or Gyra (s) are the regions between deep folds, Sulci (p) or Sulcus (s) and fissures of the brain divide the CEREBRAL CORTEX into six lobes: the FRONTAL

DARK MATTER MECHANICS

LOBE, PARIETAL LOBE, OCCIPITAL LOBE, TEMPORAL LOBE, the LIMBIC LOBE and INSULA or INSULAR CORTEX, a portion of the CEREBRAL CORTEX.

Neuroscience includes the physiology and anatomy of the brain. It is the intention to address neuroscience in that the parts of the brain that accept memories and those that store and remit them where memory is being alleged or argued being stored in the vacuum wherever it may be found. If memory is emitted as a wave in the atmosphere then it is in effect broadcasting, if in a liquid then it is also being broadcast but only wherever the liquid is found and if in a tube or wire, in this case a neuron, it is more or less a private directed distribution of a wave of information.

The CORTEX, the logic or neural network, regions of the brain are comprised at the surface a thick layer of neuronal dendrites and in the case of the CEREBAL CORTEX and the NEOCORTEX, the most dense and have the most layers, having six layers. The layers serve to refine the logic of the CORTEX database of choices and are progressively refined.

The anatomy of the brain is divided into three main structures called the CEREBRUM, CEREBELLUM and the BRAIN STEM. The CEREBRUM covers the outer surface of the brain and is segmented into eight lobes and areas and in each, various functionalities has been identified. Of these eight regions, the largest is the FRONTAL LOBE comprising approximately the front half of the CEREBRUM.

Along the surface of the CEREBRUM and the CEREBELLUM and just below is the CORTEX, a outer layer comprised of the outer surface and several layers deep is the gray matter of the CORTEX where the dendrites of neurons with ends face outward. Below the gray matter is the white layer comprised of the axons of the gray matter, separating the layers.

The FRONTAL LOBE is the largest body of the CEREBRUM behind the forehead and about halfway back. An isolated area in the FRONTAL LOBE is the BROCA AREA. Behind the FRONTAL LOBE is the MOTOR STRIP running from the surface to the lower part of the CEREBRUM. Just behind the MOTOR STRIP is the SENSORY STRIP next to the length of the motor strip. Behind and next to the SENSORY STRIP is the PARIETAL LOBE located along the upper back part of the CEREBRUM. Against to and below the back of the PARIETAL LOBE is the OCCIPITAL LOBE forming the lowermost and final lobe having an outer surface part of the CEREBRUM. The WERNICKE AREA is attached to the lower region of the PARIETAL

LOBE.

Below the body of the CEREBRUM and the WERNICKE AREA is the TEMPORAL LOBE stretching along the lower length of the CEREBRUM in contact with all the lobes and along the sides of the brain structure. The gray matter is the neuron bodies and dendrites and unmyalinated axons while the white matter is the myalinated axons. The NEOCORTEX and the gray layers of the CORTEX and NEOCORTEX, the most dense having six layers, is known as a logic system The gray matter extends to the back and below and is a much smaller structure called the CEREBELLUM is located behind the lowest part of the lobes behind the BRAINSTEM.

The most prominent and most massive structure of the brain is the outermost structure, the CEREBRUM, submerged in the fluid under the bony skull that is divided as the left and right side which communicates with each other through a structure or region called the CORPUS CALLOSUM located midway between the front and back between the left and right side of the CEBEBRUM. The left side services the right side of the body and vice verse for the right side of the CEREBRUM.

The brain has a rather complex anatomy that is

discussed with colorized images of the brain on the Web in helpful detail at https://mayfieldclinic.com/pe-anatbrain.htm by the he Mayfield Clinic and Mayfield Education & Research Foundation located in Cincinnati OH. Much of the anatomical descriptions herein were learned from this URL, but without direct quotes, using observations and functionality from common knowledge learned from other sources, much of which on the Web.

The purpose here is to attempt to isolate the parts of the brain engaged in memory storage and recall. Current literature focuses on nerve functions in controlling specific parts of the body and their sources and uses of those purposes. There are parts of the brain that is engaged in memory functions. The structures have been, presumably, stimulated in a conscious subject who is able to communicate memories that are forced to be recalled.

The CEREBRUM region of the brain is divided into the right and left hemispheres where each hemisphere controls the opposite side of the body. Together, they are the largest part of the brain that covers the top of the brain from front to back and down to the bottom back of the brain. It is the seat of intelligence and fine control of the body.

DARK MATTER MECHANICS

The outer layer and surface of the CEREBRUM, called the CORTEX, is the gray matter of the brain including the folds and other surfaces facing the inner surfaces of the skull. The outer face of the Cortex is comprised of the thickly packed dendrites of the nerve cells and below comprising the body of the CEREBRUM is the white matter comprised of the axons leading away from the dendrites of the gray matter.

The regions of gray matter are collections of dendrite tentacles, unmyalinated axons and numerous glial cells performing maintenance and many other functions in the gray matter of the brain, BRAINSTEM and SPINAL CORD.

The CEREBELLUM is a smaller mass located behind the BRAINSTEM and below the CEREBRUM and serves as a coordination center between the brain and the various muscles of the body. The CEREBRUM is a much larger region of the brain CORTEX OF THE CEREBRUM contains many neurons while the CEREBELLUM, a much smaller body, contains over four times the number of neurons. Also, the CEREBELLUM is located next to the back of the BRAINSTEM which is the uppermost part of the spinal cord into which the output of the CEREBELLUM feeds. The massive surface of the CEREBRUM and its

MEMORY, MIND AND CONSCIOUSNESS

CORTEX of gray matter is popularly known as the neural logic network where artificial computer programs are able to perform selection capabilities by recognizing and analyzing images.

The two halves of the CEREBRUM perform different functions where the LEFT HEMISPHERE is referred to as the dominant hemisphere and is responsible for speech and language. The RIGHT HEMISPHERE is generally responsible for interpreting visual images and spatial processing. These two functions may be reversed for left hander persons.

The two halves of the CEREBRUM are connected by the Corpus Callous that is comprised of nerve fibers that carry messages between the left and right part of the brain.

The Frontal lobe occupies the front half of the CEREBRUM and is responsible for personality, emotions and behavior. It plays a part in self awareness and judgment, intelligence, and concentration. The Broca's area controls understandable speaking and writing and the MOTOR STRIP is involved in body movement.

The Parietal lobe is located behind the MOTOR STRIP and SENSORY STRIP to the top back of the brain. The SENSORY STRIP interprets language and words and also is the touch and pain center. The PARIETAL LOBE is responsible for sensory and memory and its interpretation of vision, hearing and motor signals. It is responsible for spatial and visual perception. The OCCIPITAL LOBE is located below the PARIETAL LOBE at the low back of the head and interprets visual stimuli and movement.

The TEMPORAL LOBE is located to the side of the forgoing lobes with the Wernicke area connecting the TEMPORAL LOBE with the PARIETAL LOBE. It is responsible for understanding language. The BROCA'S AREA lies in the LEFT FRONTAL LOBE and controls the facial muscles and emitted sounds but when damaged Broca's aphasia results affecting speech but fails to affect the ability to read and understand language. The WERNICKE'S AREA lies in the LEFT TEMPORAL LOBE also responsible for sentences and speech unless damaged, and then Wernicke's aphasia causes nonsensical speech and lack of understanding.

The CORTEX OF THE CEREBRUM gives the outer appearance of folds and crevices that allows a greater area to exist in the same space. The raised area is called a Gyrus and the deep groove or crevice that separates each Gyrus is called a Sulcus.

MEMORY, MIND AND CONSCIOUSNESS

The Grey matter of the CORTEX is the outer or surface layer comprised of layers of nerve cells while beneath is the white matter of the CORPUS that is comprised of long nerve fibers, the axons, of the Grey matter that connects the brain areas to each other. The outer structures surround a number of significant inner structures.

Below the outer structures of the brain are more functional structures that have assigned functions. These can be grouped as six structures, The HYPOTHALAMUS, PITUITARY GLAND, PINEAL GLAND, BASAL GANGLIA, LIMBIC SYSTEM and the THALAMUS.

The THALAMUS is a midline structure of dense gray matter organizing deep sorts and disseminates information to and from the various regions of the CORTEX and NEOCORTEX and BRAINSTEM and spinal cord. It resides under fold of the CEREBRUM.

The PREFRONTAL CORTEX holds very short term memory.

The HIPPOCAMPUS (encodes long term memory, and holds long term memory).

The LIMBIC SYSTEM in the CINGULATE GYRI HYPOTHALAMUS, AMYGDALA, (emotion) and

HIPPOCAMPUS (long term memory).

The BRAINSTEM is seen to penetrate both the CEREBRUM and CEREBELLUM and connecting the SPINAL CORD. It controls many of the automatic functions of the body and facilitates communication between the brain located above it with the rest of the body below.

The HYPOTHALAMUS controls the AUTONOMIC SYSTEM regulating secretion of hormones and plays a role in controlling hunger, thirst, sleep and sexual responses and is important in regulating body temperature, blood pressure and emotions.

The PITUITARY GLAND is located at the base of the skull in a bony pocket called the SELLA TURCICA, connected to the HYPOTHALAMUS by the PITUITARY STALK. It is the master gland controlling other ENDOCRINE GLANDS and secretes hormones that control sexual development, promotes bone and muscle growth and response to stress.

The PINEAL GLAND helps regulate the internal clock and circadian rhythms by secreting melatonin and helps in sexual development.

The Thalamus is above the HYPOTHALAMUS through which virtually all information from and to the

CORTEX flows. It plays a role in pain sensation, attention, alertness and also memory.

The BASAL GANGLIA is a set of nuclei that is responsible for fine movements of the fingers working with the CEREBELLUM. Its parts include the CAUDATE, PUTAMEN and GLOBUS PALLIDUS.

The LIMBIC SYSTEM is the center of emotions, learning involving the HIPPOCAMPUS for memory and the HYPOTHALAMUS and AMYGDALA for emotional reactions. Also included are the CINGULATE GYRI, HYPOTHALAMUS,

The outer structures are surrounded by the SUBARACHNOID space that is filled with CEREBROSPINAL FLUID that separates the Grey matter from the bony skill. The inner structures are generally separated from each other by spinal fluid in named spaces, cisterns, sinuses, foramen, aqueducts and ventricles that are connected to the SUBARACHNOID SPACE. The fluid is recycled by structures in the SUPERIOR SAGITTAL SINUS called ARACHNOID VILLI.

There are two lateral ventricles within the CEREBRAL HEMISPHERES that connect to the third ventricle through a separate opening called the foramen of Monro just below the CORTEX below with the third ventricle and then through a tube called the aqueduct of Sylvius and below into the fourth ventricle and below that into the Cisterna Magna and into the central canal of the spinal cord.

The tissues of the brain, the MENINGES, are essentially only three in number.

The DURA MATER is a thick and durable membrane closest to the bone inside of the skull and vertebrae surrounding the spinal cord. It is made of elastic fiber containing spaces in two layers containing the larger blood vessels leading into the capillaries in the PIA MATER. It has a middle region that splits the DURA MATER into two layers forming a sac surrounding the large DURAL SINUSES that carries venous blood from the brain toward the heart.

The ARACHNOID MATER is a thin loosely fitting sac that is a transparent fibrous membrane with an outermost layer of tightly packed cells considered an effective barrier between the cerebrospinal fluid and the inner space. Its inner lining is a fatty tissue closer to the inner surface.

PIA MATER is the innermost membrane surrounding the brain and spinal cord made of connective tissue serving to be a protective membrane. It is a thin delicate membrane that adheres to contours the brain in the sulci and around the gyri and thought to be impermeable to fluid.

While the forgoing is likely more than anyone would like to know, the contacts between logic systems may be significant in commutating with each other using waves that emerge at the bottom of the logic systems. Also, it is apparent that physical connectors between all that use the output of the logic systems is hardly likely. More likely is the use of radio wave like waves possibly containing identifications and perhaps some sort of dating system that act as a network throughout with perhaps older systems of direct contact through the nerves.

COMMUNICATION

We know that nerve sensors populate the skin to detect the sensations of touch while deeper below the skin are nerve sensors that detect pressure and others that detect pain and send a message to a ganglia in the spinal cord to be transmitted to the brain for a reaction. In the mean time, the ganglion returns the message to pull away or some other appropriate reaction.

If one wants to communicate a statement, a complete statement is addressed to another. An incomplete statement may well be a question requiring a response to complete the statement. The incomplete statement relays the subject matter, perhaps in a broadcast, seeking in a way, opinions that answer the question. If the question is addressed to a crowd of memory and logic systems, there may be a number of answers shouted back or presented each in turn.

A simple sensor sending information to the brainstem could be called an incomplete piece of information being sent with a host of other messages sent from a host of other sensors. It is the job of the brain to put all the messages together in a logical way together with what memory can provide and determine a reasonable course of action.

The brain communicates with specific parts of itself and with specific parts of the rest of the body generally through the nerves that are in the brain, the spinal cord and the cranial nerves from the brain stem or the CEREBRUM. What should be of interest is what it is that is being transmitted. The literature generally refers to signals or pulses of electricity, electric current, meaning electrons, being supplied at one point and collected at another to form a circuit or to or from an energy source.

Some of the cranial nerves originate in the brain stem and a few others originate in the cerebrum. They are customarily listed in Roman Numerals but the numbers are as follows:

1. Smell, is a sensory nerve that detects pheromones.

2. Sight, is a sensory nerve transmits signal from the retina to the brain.

3. Moves the eye using six separate muscles for eye movements and innervates the sphincter papillae muscles of the pupil and the

cilliary body of the eye.

4. Moves the eye, innervates the superior oblique muscle that depresses, abducts and intorts the eyeball.

5. Receives sensation from the face and innervates the muscles of mastication.

6. Moves eye, innervates the lateral rectus muscle of the eye that abducts the eye.

7. Moves facial expression, innervates the digestive muscle and the stylohyoid muscle, and innervates salivary glands (not the parotid) and the lacrimal gland.

8. Hearing sound, rotation and gravity balance sensations, and equilibrium and the cochlear branch carries impulses for hearing.

9. Taste to the posterior third of the tongue. It is involved with the vagus(10) nerve in the gag reflex and innervates swallow muscles.

10.   Heart rate, lung and digestive track.

11.   Moves head using the sternocleidomastoid and the trapezius muscles

MEMORY, MIND AND CONSCIOUSNESS

12.   Moves   tongue   using   the
palatoglossal   muscle   important   in   swallowing
and manage speech articulation.

The EEG waves pass through the skull and the MENINGES around the brain are compression waves in the vacuum, not flow of electrons but may be waves the size of electrons or photons.   If electricity is electrons taken from the atoms of the circuitry, chemical reactions should, but do not, take place. Brainwaves can therefore carry information as ordinary compression waves in ways we do not yet understand, simply because theorists insist the vacuum cannot actively participate in wave structure in the frequencies of brainwaves allowing the lobes, to in effect, talk to each other.

Electricity and electrical current is not flow of electrons as the empty vacuum presumption requires but vacuum atmosphere of particles in and around the atoms allow current to be vacuum compression waves, not electrons.

There are no obvious pathways or circuitry in the anatomy of the brain described here through which electrical current can be flowing, other than the insulated nerve fibers or circulatory system, though a possibility, as electrons, but waves in the vacuum as ordinary compression waves can bypass the hardwired circuitry required to service the needs of the body.

Waves in general are addressed liberally in the theoretical subject of literature inexplicably passing through the empty vacuum such as the brainwaves. The literature does not state that these waves are electromagnetic light waves. Light does not pass through bone and layers of tissue that protect the brain but compression waves with minute variations that carry information to be stored in the dedicated lobes as memory to be used according to the purposes of the lobes do.

Electromagnetic waves are uniform strands of quantum sized waves and in theory, the only information they can carry is the frequency of the sinusoidal shape. Pulses of vacuum material that have internal structure likely can be like a snapshot with variations in the images and where wavelengths are detected, it is likely sequential images are directly interpreted as sequences of images conveying movement from one image to another like a movie. These are likely or could be the same types of waves that are viewed as electric current when detected being passed out of the atmosphere and into the nervous system without processing.

ABSTRACTION

Theorists have completely ignored or skirted the need to understand the vacuum as a substance by regarding it as empty space and presuming that all behavior that actually occurs in the vacuum are attributes of observable particles of mass. Where waves are detected, they are assigned the property of being independent particles because ordinary compression waves are not possible in empty space. Particle vacuum being discussed here is not the aether gas but rather the vacuum itself that is comprised of an infinite range of particle sizes constructed without any space but rather are in structures that allow the vacuum to behave as expected, and more.

The process of focusing on one aspect of a problem while ignoring other aspects is what is known as abstraction or abstracting away the clutter of parts of reality while focusing on another. The concept of a standing aether gas in the empty space was set aside by theorists while focusing on other aspects of physics just over one hundred year ago requiring abandonment of the concept of causation for physical phenomenon in physics. The presumption of empty vacuum could be called simplification where the process of abstraction is generally when other parts are understood but omitted.

The aether theory was abandoned just over one hundred years ago with the failure of proof of an expected property. As a result, theorists simply adopted the convention of pretending that the vacuum lacks any substance without explaining the fields and other properties that form in the vacuum. Without a full understanding, the abstract may be the entirety of what was known a century ago.

The aether was regarded as the luminiferous aether responsible for the transmission of light waves and believed to be a standing gas through which all movement passes. Scientists theorized that a moving object would experience an aether wind and that if the relative velocity of the aether wind could be measured then the velocity of the moving object could be absolutely determined by its effect on the speed of light. The theory was that if a beam of light were to be facing head on into the wind, the velocity would be measurable as a minimum and if in the opposite direction then the velocity would be at a maximum, and variable in other directions. There would be no way of knowing which was which but if the angles are different then there would at least be a difference in the measured velocity.

The thought was that the speed of the wind would affect the speed of light if ever so slightly and the experiment could proceed using a split beam of light and pass both beams through an interferometer and the difference in velocity would be seen if one passed through the interferometer at slightly different times then the difference would be noticeable and experiment would be a success.

Very precise experiments were carried out, now called the Michelson-Morley experiments, comparing the time a split beam of light aimed in different directions and brought back in alignment using mirrors were compared to determine the differences. Both beams arrived at the same time establishing that the theory involving the expected nature of the aether gas interacting with light was erroneous.

The experiment drew the attention of Albert Einstein and one of his collaborators, Ernst Mach who at the time was involved in measuring the speed of accelerated particles compared to the speed of sound, now known for by his name, responsible for the Mach unit for measuring velocities compared to the speed of sound even today. Mach was skeptical of whether there were even particles in the vacuum or whether physics could address them, if they were. Einstein was skeptical about whether the speed of light could ever be changed by the means of the experiment.

Einstein had predicted before the experiment was carried out that the velocity of light would be the same, under the condition now well known, if measured in the same inertial frame as the light. Mach was known to be the last scientist to admit that even the air was filled with molecules, though already proven to be the case, on the grounds that they are not observable. Whether it was on grounds of philosophical arguments claiming that it could be ignored as a matter of scientific expedience or simply as matter disbelief is unclear. Einstein was known to be of the belief that the vacuum had to comprise matter as being necessary in measuring distance in the vacuum, but he had argued that regardless of the wind, there would be no way to change the speed of light. As a theorist, he had no reason to explain why that would be the case but it is likely that t he speed of waves are a property of the medium.

Mach is known to be responsible for the establishment of the concept of the empty vacuum contrary to Einstein's arguments, and even after the experiments, Einstein in a presentation openly acknowledged that the vacuum is probably not, in reality, empty but disagreed with the aether theory with regard to the predictions. They both agreed that the presumption of empty vacuum was philosophically appropriate, at least for purposes of mathematics.

Some argue the Michelson-Morley result was due to aether drag such that the instruments or the entire laboratory captured the aether and drug it along so that it may have been no aether wind within the region of the experiment. This argument does not seek to contradict the way the experiment was carried but that there was no aether wind. That the drag completely nullifies the aether wind under the conditions of the experiment since the experiment was meant to measure the wind effect.

The empty vacuum presumption was accepted throughout the scientific community, whether because it was true or because it could be ignored as a matter of philosophical expedience, as an acceptable expediency in a reality that may cause loss of focus if all the clutter of reality were always addressed, a process now known as abstraction. It was never intended to be known as a matter of fact, but rather a presumption. If the Michelson-Morley result was accepted as proof of the empty vacuum

The presumption is still being honored in physics today, even though it creates a whole host of inexplicable properties that are not accounted for in physics or theoretical physics directly due to the presumption. Light was already known as being waves in the presumed luminiferous aether but the wave concept for electromagnet waves being an extraordinary sort of wave attributable largely to Einstein by interpreting the experiments of the day as photon particles comprising the wave shaped as a sinusoidal structure that travels through empty space.

Quantum mechanics was being formulated at the time of Einstein who suggested that the quantum theory supported the concept of duality of particles-matter that was believed to be a property of photons depending on the experiment where the photon behaved as a particle and in others it behaved as a wave. The duality of photons was carried forward for all particles having the duality property. The mathematics describing the property was completed and a Nobel Prize for the proof was awarded accordingly.

If the presumption of empty vacuum were to have been replaced by the presumption that the vacuum is a material medium, it might have been determined that in it a compression wave could behave as a particle where a particle was required or a wave otherwise. It could be that the Nobel Prize fixed the presumption as a matter of fact and the inexplicable duality behavior. The quantum sized compression wave could explain the mathematical results.

Einstein has been attributed the "spooky action at a distance" expression which some take to mean that he supported the empty vacuum presumption, though maybe not. It was said regarding quantum entanglement in which two associated particles could be separate, even at great distances, and they could still communicate their state or changes in state, a behavior that to this day remains inexplicable.

One might imagine that all of physics is filled with many inexplicable actions at a distance in view of the use of the presumption of empty vacuum. The familiar properties described in physics such as gravity and magnetism are not convincingly explained in terms of mechanisms that are involved and even energy itself remains inexplicable notwithstanding its use throughout physics as though it is the cause of much behavior. Energy is a behavior and in that regard, all of physics and theoretical physics are all about behavior even though often used as expressions of causation.

DARK MATTER MECHANICS

A phenomenon is regarded as unexplained in physics if the behavior has not been described satisfactorily using a proof based on mathematics generally requiring a means for measuring the phenomenon. There are numerous expressions that describe behaviors such as "energy" or behavior attributed to energy that in reality only describe when energy is known to be present and quantifiable such as if a mass is accelerated. "Force" is another expression that is quantifiable by the amount of movement of a mass but in physics, a science that based on observable behavior, the cause is generally well known as an observed object passing is movement on to another mass.

The words that are used physics where the cause of the movement, for instance, is not stated, should be regarded as an abstraction, even though in physics the cause can usually be determined, are well defined as how to calculate the behavior rather defined by attribution to a specific cause.

While it was quantum entanglement and quantum mechanics in general that baffled Einstein, physics was already abandoning "cause and effect" but fully invested in "action reaction" physics where an action equals the inverse of its reaction as the basis of the equations that are used in physics.

MEMORY, MIND AND CONSCIOUSNESS

Generally, theories are abstractions of reality where focus is on one or two properties in disregard of much of the rest that could be addressed or is addressed in another theory. It may take many abstractions to complete a model of a given segment of reality. The success of physics is based on abstractions but where a problem could be about the velocity of a known object and an equation addressing a general object is both an abstraction and often referred as a generalization.

While there may be many abstract theories about some reality, leaving much to be explained elsewhere, though not always is somewhere else to be found. Models used to illustrate some mathematical description are also an abstraction that is never claimed to represent the underlying complete reality. The empty vacuum presumption has never been described as a matter of fact, or to be provable, but all theorists and physicists are compelled to respect it in their new discoveries and theories in order to be consistent other theories.

Since the failure of the Michelson-Morley experiment, the experiment has been conducted by many others while refining the procedures with generally the same result. There has been reluctance among physicists to indulge in theoretical mechanics resulting in that branch of science becoming known as only addressing observable or clearly detectable phenomena, leaving theories to the mathematicians of theoretical physics. As a result of that decision, physics has benefited by the conclusion it addresses, are regarded as being factual in nature and not just theories, due to its findings always being based on observability.

The empty vacuum presumption seems like an unfinished project in theoretical physics, perhaps thought to be addressed at some future time. The empty vacuum presumption has not been addressed in physics or theoretical physics leaving many unaddressed issues as inexplicable phenomena. The vacuum is responsible for virtually all behavior requiring theorists to skirt around the issues by attaching much of the known behavior to some particle of mass, such as the fields, but have no basis for them to exist since mass alone would be inert material.

Theoretical physics has resorted to a mathematical abstraction of energy as the fundamental basis for all reality. Energy is a description of a behavior or potential behavior but theorists have been using it as a cause for behavior. The abstraction has never been completed by describing just what it is that is behaving, as when in the big bang theory, mass is claimed to have been created due to the high velocities of energy.

The same is true force fields where force is defined as movement but most presume there is a cause but it is not the presence of forces alone, where causation must exist in the vacuum that is presumed empty, resulting in theorists proclaiming that causation is no longer necessary and possibly never existed. In practice, a force is transfer of momentum through contact and the contact is usually describe in practice leaving little doubt what caused it.

The failure of the theoretical model is to abandon the project, leaving it in an incomplete state. Perhaps delving into the vacuum as a project was too daunting or complex for the mathematics of the time in hopes that someday a mathematical solution would present itself. When asked the feared question, which is always asked for the answer to what causes the described behavior, the response Is invariably that it will take some time to determine, perhaps even years or decades, which will be true so long as the erroneous presumption of empty vacuum remains in effect.

Once a presumption of material vacuum is adopted, the issue of causation solves virtually all the questions about causation. The ordinary compression wave will become obvious and many of the named particles will obviously be determined to be compression wave peaks where we perhaps live in the trough of these faux particles. Many of the compression waves persist like wrinkles in a bed sheet that is too large for the bed, and will remain persistent until the vacuum is thinned out by the expansion of the universe. When that happens, the physics of today will cease to function.

Force fields are an abstraction in which there is no answer to the remaining reality in our theories due primarily to the empty vacuum presumption. When answered, energy will become known as the compression waves moving objects at the particle level and gravity and magnetic fields will be known as gradient fields in which particles and objects move either toward or away from the vacuum density in a gradient according to the principles of buoyancy. The mathematics already exists if only it is used in the solution that must be sought using terms such as pressure and density changes and differences in the vacuum.

The state of the vacuum may be virtually free of friction due to layers of smaller and smaller lubricating particles but it is the vacuum pressure that drives and maintains the wave and gravity structures which will persist so long as the universe remains a dense vacuum container or is constantly being renewed, perhaps as a function of black holes, consuming mass and converting it to vacuum.

Electromagnetic waves are strings of quantum sized common compression waves emitted in sequence to form the sinusoidal shape theoretically by orbiting electron or perhaps by spinning sources or even emissions traveling up and down a proton's Faraday tube extending out of the proton envelope causing the familiar planar polarized light. Much larger waves can and do exist with gradients between the peaks and troughs able to attract and hold masses having volume that displaces an equal amount of vacuum. Vacuum being a liquid form of matter containing no empty space whatsoever, its density equals that of mass, the solid measurable form of matter, where vacuum and mass are both comprised of atomistic structures of cores and their gradients while containing no empty space whatsoever.

Energy is measured by the acceleration of mass on which energy is acting but argued herein to be the waves that push particles. While waves are able to cause objects of mass to move, a description of a distant behavior must still be described that has caused the wave to exist. Theory is universally understood to ne based on a mathematical proof. The intention here is to trace behavior to a mechanical cause where contact between objects will pass motion from one particle in the vacuum to another and should be called a mechanical theory as opposed to a mathematical theory.

SCIENCE

E nergy is a named theoretical abstraction that describes movement in the vacuum but wholly fails to specify the mechanisms of what causes the movement. In studies of quantum mechanics of electromagnetic light waves, it has been determined that energy comes in small quantum photon packets and as no other form. It was energy that was emitted during the big bang that resulted in the creation of all that comprises the universe, according to the Big Bang Theory.

Notwithstanding the experimental fact that particles of all sizes are accompanied by a wave packet or plane wave, here argued to drive the momentum of the particle, all of which is precisely set out in mathematical form and, as always, the presumption that the vacuum is empty space so that the mechanism cannot be explained but the behavior can be described. The theory explaining the phenomenon arises out of quantum mechanics and the wave is referred to as the matter wave or the De Broglie hypothesis describing the duality nature of moving particles having wave-particle nature of moving particles.

The mathematics of matter waves is a combination of the findings of various physicists and theoretical physicists, building on the quantum mechanical theory (mathematics) the accuracy of which is not questioned here but replication of the results are stated here, without proof, are possible as a mechanical causation only if the vacuum is realized as a material medium, possibly such as that described herein.

Every particle possesses gravitational properties which is the gradient structure of the atomistic particle surrounding the largest central core of the particle. A wave in the medium is the core being forced to move forward by the contact and transfer of motion in formation of the wave. The core moves no further than the size of its gradient which pushed aside allowing the core to push the neighboring particle in the direction of the wave forward, after which the cores and their gradients return to their former state.

The duration of the cores contact depends on the amplitude of the wave which increases until the wave peak is constructed whereupon the vacuum cores can begin returning to their original state as the trough of the wave is approached which may be the state of the vacuum before passage of the wave as with the quantum wave. It is possible that a less dense state be created than the original density of the vacuum if the original motion is pulled back beyond its original position to construct a trough that pulls the impacting particles past its original position until less density is reached, whereupon the particles regain the original shape as the vacuum regains its original density with respect to the core particles as the trough is deconstructed.

The forgoing behavior is much like a wave construction in a molecular medium but where the molecules generally only get closer together in a wave peak unless the wave is very powerful. The molecular atmosphere is made of a number of different molecules which could cause a wave to misbehave, indicating that it is possible that the waves of molecular particles are in reality due to the waves created in the vacuum.

As the wave approaches a fixed barrier, the momentum of the wave is the movement of the core that is next to the barrier and if the core is able to penetrate the barrier then the next wave peak will be deconstructed by being spread about while the cores continue to penetrate the barrier replicating the sinusoidal shape of the wave within the barrier, especially when the barrier is the envelope of a proton belonging to an atom as a compression wave has momentum enough to penetrate the envelope.

In theory, electricity in a circuit will force the electrons of the medium out of their location due to the vacuum pressures but it is the vacuum that is the current that generally takes the form of waves, the theoretical energy. Potential is pressure that is compressed within a circuit by accepting an augmentation of compressed vacuum when generated by being passed through a strong magnetic gradient enhanced by coiled wire with current passing through it at a generator station. Various well known means for increasing the potential in a circuit but what should be true is that electric current is not electrons being pushed out of their proton envelope but rather perhaps expansion of the envelopes.

The concept of electrons as current was a concept created out of necessity to find a particle in a theoretical presumption of empty space. Tearing an electron from the envelope of its proton would cause disruption to the structure of the medium of the circuit or affect the fabric of a biological medium when in a neuron, creating many charged particles that do not exist.

Inputs into the brain from the outside take the form of waves, through the eyes and ears and so are those that are created within the brain as its input and after processing is generally stored as concepts requiring a great number of facts that must be kept together as in a proton envelope. The wave material and its structure can be moved from one location to another allowing further processing.

The huge number of neurons and their dendrites are likely enough to control the muscles and endocrine system and other sundry gland secretions and provide the logic used in the layers comprising the neuron network of the gray matter. The lower lifeforms need less body control due to their simple needs but the size of the brain or whatever nervous systems they possess needs little space to be functional if the thought systems are in the atoms rather than the complex nervous system if the functions are as being described herein.

Because the processes are properties of the physics, minus the mathematics, the evolutions of the species are not accidental but rather compelled or inevitable. As more body behavior must be controlled through the nervous system, as more functionality is added there is a concurrent addition to the nervous system reaching the size and capacity of the human brain. The evidence is clear of the evolutionary process by examination of the classification of the evolving species of both plant and animal kingdoms.

If the processes of the nervous system and perhaps the chemistry itself of the biological system as a whole is the product of the complexity of the atom rather than the atom having the simple description of physicists only able to absorb and emit light and use energy to increase or decrease orbit diameter of electrons, is being just complex enough to produce the evidence of it existence. The atoms must cooperate in the functions of lifeforms such that new life is inevitable.

In the process of reciting the evidence of describing behavior while abandoning one of the most important tenants of physics, that of cause and effect, an important law of physics and clue regarding the nature of the single most dominant and ubiquitous regions in the entire universe, the vacuum. The vacuum behaves as a medium in many ways, particularly in the fields that are described in theoretical physics that exist in the vacuum. Cosmology has almost established that the dark matter is vacuum, though a redundant proof if established.

All that was needed was to look back at the single weakest and most unnecessary of all the unproven presumptions of physics, that with the least amount of reflection regarding all the inexplicable behaviors, understanding the vacuum would be seen to be an important evolution of the science. Rather than accepting the challenge of discovering mechanisms of how things work, the move was made to describe only the objects and their behavior, a very different and less potent occupation.

Physics began as a science with a keen sense of what can be observed about nature while keeping notes of measurements and relationships to keep observations precise while theoretical physics had the much different purpose, that of developing and advancing the mathematical sciences by using the measurements and relationships of physics. Had theoretical physics been named more appropriately as theoretical mathematics, physics may have continued on its unique mission.

Apparently, physics evolved into a mathematical science leaving the physical sciences unattended. If we look back on all the discoveries held to be in physics, we find that they are all in the mathematics of physical behavior. Gravity is not the discovery that apples fall or about the mechanisms or mechanical causes of gravity but rather how to calculate the rates that apples fall resulting in the mathematical discovery of the calculus.

DARK MATTER MECHANICS

Einstein used the concept and calculation of curvature in his field equations of relativity rather than principals of physics or mechanics. Most important of all is the approach taken by Albert Einstein in ignoring physics by using strictly calculations of behavior now being followed as the preferred method of approaching physics. The preferred approach to the atom and behavior of the electrons is based on the mathematics of wave functions. Faraday discovered magnetic lines of force was a physics concept that was converted into a mathematical calculation, perhaps leading away from the true nature of the atom.

It might be said that physics evolved in its movement toward mathematics and away from physics when the primary purpose of physics is to imagine or construct behavior and let the mathematicians determine how it should be calculated.

Brain science has been primarily focused on the anatomy of the macro structures and micro structures of the tissues rather than seeking to understand the physics of the vacuum, but then the vacuum has uniformly been held to be of no substance and of no significance which is a problem that can be traced directly to theorists.

The total lack of understanding the nature of

waves in the atmosphere has been focused entirely on the electromagnet waves where wavelength is a spacial distance from one extreme point to the next when the common compression wave also has a wavelength that is the distance from a maximum density to the next maximum density where the peaks and troughs are often confused between one and the other. The vacuum was overlooked in seeking compression wave peaks and troughs by the existence of the empty vacuum presumption.

The fault is also due to the focus on the polarization of waves which does not exist for compression waves. Polarization is a fact that supported the theory of the orbiting electrons emitting the photons drawing a sinusoidal wave in the vacuum traveling at the speed of light. There are other ways that the wave can be formed such as a spinning atom spewing photons or a straight antenna emitting waves up and down its length just as radio waves are created as sinusoidal waves when extracted by a receiver.

Polarization is not necessarily a natural state of waves since allowing light to pass through a polarizing device filters out some of the light while serving to polarize the light that is allowed to pass through. To the extent that polarization of light supports the orbiting electron and the responsibility is placed on the electron for emitting photons or even the quantum compression wave of energy as argued herein, one must ask why a second look at the issue of orbiting electrons should not be reevaluated.

The orbiting electron model was based largely on the orbiting planets as a model and the convenience of the readymade mathematics for calculating those orbits and later the accuracy of the mathematics of orbiting objects in gravity fields may have in some way seemed to support the concept as applied to the atom.

Another issue that the empty vacuum has perhaps caused error in concept may be in quantum mechanics where the duality of mass is based largely on the waves that have been proven experimentally to accompany the particles. Tt may well be, as is being argued herein, that the waves are present along with the presence of the particles in association with each other rather than particles having dual properties. The wave may cause the behavior in one instance while the particle works in another, a different proposition than the dual property explanation.

As the energy that is measured in the light waves as electromagnetic waves, it is when light strikes a light meter, the energy is filtered through atoms in the meter which emits the energy in light that is the sum of the separate quantum compression waves that is related to the spacial wave peaks and troughs which at best is confusing.

INFINITY

Proof of infinity as boundlessness has been a part of mathematics for centuries with regard to counting an infinite set using the real numbers. Many regard infinity as a theory that is not likely to apply to anything that exists in reality, particularly since numbers are an abstraction that only applies to reality when addressing reality and when bumped up against in calculations is regarded as an error even though liberally used in calculus.

The proof of infinity, simply put, resides in the real numbers where for any number there exists yet another number that is larger or smaller without limit. An extension of the concept is the possibility of infinity of infinities and distinguishing one infinity from another or that one may be more or less populated than another.

The particles are all accompanied by a gravity field and sometimes a magnetic field, herein referred to as atomistic structures, both of which are described herein as gradients made of infinitesimally smaller atomistic particles allowing the functionality of the vacuum by reducing or eliminating friction where the smaller particles serve to lubricate the vacuum. The fields are comprised of atomistic particles for the same reason, total lack of friction in the vacuum due to the small particles.

The atomistic particles, meaning that they each have a vacuum structure of relatively infinitesimally small atomistic particles, and so on for atomistic particles made of atomistic particle where there is no end to the recursive repetition of finding ever smaller particles The same could be said of the repetition of large objects requiring ever larger objects from black holes holding galaxies together to the possibility that one is required to hole the universe together and so on as more universes will be found.

Particles are categorized by the size and mass of their core particle but they each have an atomistic structure of the gradient vacuum structure comprised of atomistic particles which could be a category of infinite sizes and numbers. By being atomistic particles in the gradients, they also have a category of particles that comprise their gradients of vacuum atomistic particles as yet another infinitesimal category of particles.

The cores and their gradients are two categories of particles that are comprised of an infinite variety of sizes which exists at each level of particles serving not only into the infinitesimal the vacuum but the same occurs in the observable infinitely large where the cores define the size. An example are the planets where the small atoms and their molecules are larger nearer the core and the atmosphere is an extension where large particles of air is closer to the surface and thinner as the outer space is approached.

The atoms have a nuclear core and a gradient that allows the core to exist buoyantly in a higher level where the planetary core holds the planet together. The stars hold the planets together in orbits and the black hole of galaxies hold the galaxies together. Some stars are seen to have expanded and then collapsed ending in a violent explosion leaving a category of bodies that are the dwarf stars left behind after a star explodes.

Theorists have concluded that the dwarf star category of stars are created by the implosion of a preceding star but it is likely that the dwarf star existed and took part in the formation of the following star and each star could have a dwarf star as its core solving many of the perplexing issues of how stars and planets are formed. For the planets, a dwarf star may have suffered some damage when the star imploded allowing particles of the very dense matter to be spread throughout the universe. We have no sure way to determine what the core of our planet is made of other than assuming elemental metal atoms are accumulated there.

It is known that if a piece of a dwarf star material the size of a pea were to land on the planet, the Earth's crust could not support its existence on the surface and it would immediately sink into the planet and perhaps even to the core due to its super density. If such material were to reach the Sun, it would likely exist in orbit where material would be collected in formation of a planet due to its super dense gravity. If in the core, the gradient field around such a dense material would likely push the ordinary matter away due to the low density of the elements seeking a location of equal density and perhaps enlarge the planet rather than pull the material inward where there would be nowhere to go perhaps opening a space for its super dense molecules, if any.

If dwarf star material is floating about throughout the universe, at any time during the existence of the planet Earth and joins the core material of the planet, the upper tectonic plates could split into the various continents and islands as perhaps in fact did happen in the history of the planet. https://www.youtube.com/watch?v=3HDb9ljynfo The concept is illustrated by the artwork of Neal Atoms with its illustrations of the separations and shapes of the continents of Earth, its Moon and Mars at the URL. He puts forth a theory that is different than the one set out herein for the expansion of the planet's size but the illustrations are very convincing that the Earth is and has been expanding.

Theory for the creation of the dwarf star was during the collapse of its star but if the dwarf star existed before its star were created, it would have attracted material from space around it and been active in creation of the star. Its existence during the collapse of the star would have likely created parts of the dwarf star material to break off and fly into space in all directions perhaps causing creation of star nurseries that are seen around locations where an obvious explosion of a previous star and collections of stellar dust exists and young stars are seen.

A better explanation might be that the superdense dwarf star and its growing pressures within the star could have used the vacuum itself to create the core material of the atoms. Apparently, the growth of the protons and neutrons of the atoms grew under the conditions of the core responsible for the star's creation, stopping at a point when the gravitational and magnetic gradient fields were created to stop further growth by buoyantly moving to a region of less density and pressures as an explanation for why these nucleon particles are all the same size and weight.

The Sun is a normal size star, if not on the smallish side, but we know that protons and neutrons comprise the solar winds that do not penetrate the protective magnetic, or gradient, field of our planet but the Sun is apparently manufacturing and emitting Hydrogen atoms even today without waiting for its ultimate demise, but as for the larger atoms larger than Iron and after that, they must wait theoretically, until the star's collapse due to a limit in size that the star can produce within its intense atmosphere.

The core particles of the atomistic particles are perhaps super dense without their buoyant atmosphere of gradient material. Arguably, there is a gap in particle sizes from the vacuum particles to the electrons and nucleon particles of the atoms in the progression of material sizes that leaves a huge gap between the sizes of nucleons and above. The missing superdense particles in the universe that are larger than the nucleons but smaller than the dwarf stars that can be identified up to the black holes of the galaxies, could exist but remain hidden by the material they have collected around them, such as might be the cores of the moons, planets, and stars, where the range can only be counted by the size of their collected material.

There are stars being born on a regular basis but not just anywhere, rather in specific locations in the so called incubation or nursery regions where the birth of new stars are being witnessed. These locations are invariably in locations where there is evidence of a previous collapse and ultimate explosion of a star where perhaps there was a destruction of the core dwarf star yielding material of the sizes suitable for creation of new stars.

The vacuum itself is a quandary regarding its creation. At the event of the Big Bang, theorists follow the progression of energy that the event must have emitted but the physics, if the concepts herein are correct, was well in place at the time evidencing an older more mature universe that existed well before the Big Bang. In other words, a universe that surrounds our universe with a well developed mature vacuum in place for use in our universe may exist.

The full range of vacuum particles must exist within the universe before the vacuum can function properly according to the mechanical theory set forth herein, perhaps requiring more time to develop than the creation of our universe. Theorists use only the energy in the vacuum as evidence of its presence but cosmologists and astrophysicists have introduced, or reintroduced, the concept of matter into the equation of our reality. If the dark energy and dark matter are present as vacuum, the theoretical both dark energy and dark matter of the universe could be the gradient fields of the cores of the particles comprising the matter of the universe that satisfy both concepts.

The gravity of the matter comprising the universe is theoretically attempting to pull the mass of the universe into a collapse but the dark energy of the universe works against the gravity theoretically to prevent a collapse into a singularity. The dark energy is pulling the matter of the universe apart in the theoretical expansion being in evidence by the red shift in light coming from all directions. The dark energy is the energy that seeks to cause the universe to expand but without any notion of the mechanisms that may be involved on either account.

The dark matter is generally being addressed herein but the dark energy must be a part of the same process but perhaps an injection of more vacuum from other sources might cause expansion. A possible generator of vacuum is likely the processes of the black holes, pulling mass into its grinding properties and producing vacuum as its output that is likely the material that is noticed being ejected at their poles.

DARK MATTER MECHANICS

The vacuum produced by way of black holes would not cause expansion of the universe since matter is not being created nor is there any evidence that vacuum is being forcefully injected from outside the universe that could be causing the expansion.

On a brighter note, perhaps what is being noticed as evidence of expansion is the expansion that occurred at some time in the history of the universe or the red shift of light is evidence of another property of the universe, other than that the emitters of the light moving away as has been the accepted theory as evidence of the expanding universe. One would hope that by this time in the history of the universe, equilibrium of influx of vacuum material has been reached with the amount that may be being lost where the more recent events are not as evidenced by looking back into the past. The red shift first noticed by Hubble was in theoretical empty space where nothing could be causing the change in color but in material vacuum, it could be anything.

The dark energy that theorists have discovered that is preventing the gravitational pull among the bodies of the universe is being countered by the dark energy which theorists have attributed to the expansion event being forecast. If the gravity field is the gradient structures of the atomistic particles and there is no empty space that would allow forces to cause a collapse or growth in size, as one might image would be the capabilities of empty spaces, then the inability of expansion would be present other than by injection of new vacuum from the parent universe that surrounds our universe.

We can note that objects tend to expand when heated or injected with energy but it is difficult to imagine any heat source that is not emitting light waves, a fact that was noted in black body experiments. The expansion must be the injection of new vacuum into expanding objects that can even cause molecular structures to break apart.

If the vacuum is nothing as presumed in the empty vacuum presumption, then nothing would happen when heat is applied since heat is an increase in wave activity due to injection of energy, in the form of waves of vacuum material, causing molecules to become mobile and agitated. light waves are a series of quantum sized vacuum waves being emitted from over expanded proton envelopes, as discussed herein, emitted by spinning atoms or molecules caused by the emission of waves from an antenna structure of the proton envelope. A compression wave does not cause reduction in the volume of vacuum since the cores are closer together by pushing their gradients aside.

DARK MATTER MECHANICS

If we live in infinity then we cannot be anywhere near the outer or inner end since infinities have no ends. Ours would include any parent universes or theirs, for that matter, but what happens within it, the evidence must exist from somewhere that is not the beginning since there is no beginning, The beginning of our universe is evidenced by many properties that have been discovered but and end by expansion may not be the end if the mechanical theory that is set out herein is correct, on a positive note.

ENERGY

E nergy is theoretically a description of motion and is regarded as the most fundamental of all that the universe is made primarily because for subatomic particles, it is their motion that can be identified. While theorists do not claim to know where the energy came from other than from the origin of the universe, the Big Bang, but all that energy in our universe is no more or no less than that contained in the point of energy of the Big Bang. Notwithstanding, energy is also theoretically held to be neither created nor destroyed, meaning that it is conserved.

As with all theories in theoretical physics, the theories are defined in proofs seeking to describe a behavior as a mathematical proof accompanied by a model intended to illustrate the mathematical expressions in the proof. The nature of theoretical discoveries and their proofs, the evidence on point is addressed and all else is disregarded, as in abstraction as discussed herein in the section on ABSTRACTION. It is quite apparent that nothing of relevance has been assigned to the vacuum or theorists have been able to disregard evidence that of the vacuum as a causative element, such as force or energy.

The Big Bang theory seeks to trace all the matter to the original energy of the Big Bang where mass was a conversion of acceleration based on the experimental findings that mass increases when accelerated. In those experiments, a particle must be the starter mass on which the new mass is added. That notwithstanding, not only is the mass created in the big bang but all other forms of energy now present is theoretically originated in the Big Bang. Just what it is that is accelerated, in that energy is not defined as a material, it is the vacuum that is energy.

The descriptions in the proofs in theoretical physics must address some new and never before described specific behavior without addressing all the factors that may be involved, meaning that it is all treated theoretically as an abstraction, containing only the specific behavior then being addressed while addressing other relevant behaviors, if any, by citation to works of the author and when it was published. All other matters not cited are regarded as irrelevant to the topic at hand, and it fails to lead to a full understanding.

Theorists fail to address the vacuum in regard to the Big Bang but speak of forces as though the physics knows the definition and the same for energy generally defined as acceleration of a mass over a fixed distance. Einstein's famous equation for energy was a modified form of that in tha

t units of length and acceleration can be rewritten as velocity squared but It should be noted that mass is a key part of the definition.

The significance of the vacuum and energy and even the atoms being created by the big bang is one way of approaching a subject that is not yet fully understood so that the fundamentals are being addressed here due to the possibility that something of relevance was missed. The addition of particles in vacuum should not change anything about the Big Bang theory other than a comment about the vacuum.

All theoretical proofs honor the presumption of empty vacuum and not only is no mention of vacuum generally made but is deliberately avoided in their description of the discovery. There is also no mention of what could be causing the behavior, unless as an aside, because there is no requirement for addressing any causation underlying the behavior in the proof.

Energy, if ever, is discussed by the behavior that may be involved in the discovery, being attributed to energy described in the proof and may be quantified by measurement of the behavior being attributed to energy. An activity is generally in terms of acceleration or potential behavior as the energy that was necessary in creation of the potential energy and possibly the trigger that will activate or convert it from potential to kinetic energy.

Kinetic energy is generally defined in any number of ways either as momentum in vector form or a sum of motion in a space. Energy is quantified in terms suitable to the theoretical mathematical description that allows it to be inserted into the mathematics being used generally which is usually motion which is acceleration of a particle or object.

Albert Einstein chose to modify the definition of energy from acceleration times the distance of the acceleration times the mass being accelerated to a modified equivalent by an allowed moving of the mathematical terms of acceleration to that of mass times velocity squared. The units of acceleration is distance divided by time squared which when multiplied by the distance term for energy, the definition becomes distance squared divided by time squared so that distance times acceleration becomes his very famous term as velocity squared allowing energy to be defined in terms of velocity.

In this form, Einstein established that mass and energy are equivalent based on the discovery that acceleration of a particle of mass will increase the amount of mass in the particle. His very famous equation expresses the amount of energy in a mass as being the mass times the speed of light squared which is a huge amount of energy. Einstein was possibly the first to contemplate the meaning of the energy term as a mass and in the general form of the equation can be interpreted as the amount of acceleration the mass had undergone in terms of its present velocity based on the amount of mass that had been added due to acceleration.

Einstein's equation expresses the behavior of a mass as its velocity or acceleration in terms of the additional mass that is added as a result of acceleration or present velocity but wholly fails to stipulate the mechanism involved in the presence of energy such as what causes the increase in mass or what drives the acceleration or velocity as used in his theories of relativity. This is characteristic of theoretical physics, using terms of behavior but failing to determine what causes the behavior of motion when energy is present.

Other theorists were attempting to reach similar results as Einstein's theories of relativity using the aether that was thought to exist in the vacuum but Einstein was able to state the theory using only mathematics, without reference to any causation, which is the favored approach of theorists today, avoiding any mention of what in the vacuum could be causing the behavior, furthering the presumption of empty vacuum, implying that the vacuum was irrelevant in theoretical physics.

Physics adopted mathematics as a way of precisely describing behavior but also the mass but in physics, the discussion is about an observable object of mass allowing that fact to be abstracted away by referring to the object simply as an amount of mass. Three key definitions set out by Newton are the three laws of motion as follows:

> Newton's first law of motion states that an amount of mass once set in motion will remain in its motion in a straight line until acted upon by an external force.

> Newton's second law is a little more involved where it relates acceleration to the amount of force that is applied placing it in motion and the mass of the object that is accelerated as related to

force.

Newton's third law states that for every action there is an equal but opposite reaction. This law is the basis for the extensive use of equations used in physics.

These three laws are sometimes set out mathematically but are expressed in terms of behavior in relation to forces and acceleration while the first is the basis on which the presumption of empty vacuum relies.

By replacing the presumption of empty vacuum with a presumption that vacuum as a material medium, many inexplicable phenomena in physics are resolved. One property that may be determined is that the vacuum will support the formation of compression waves whereas the empty vacuum cannot. Motion of particles of all sizes have experimentally been determined to have an associated wave whereas the wave-particle duality is related to the studies growing out of quantum mechanics based on studies of the nature of electromagnet waves in empty vacuum.

The waves associated with light waves is decidedly not described in theory as compression or density waves but rather like the peaks and troughs of linked quantum or photon particles in the shape of a sinusoidal structure, often compared to the waves on the surface of water whereas density waves are beneath the surface of waves in the water that are density or pressure differences, like the common ordinary waves of molecular particles in a particle medium that cannot exist in empty vacuum.

As awesome as the mind and body are, we tend to give the mechanisms attributions that simply are not warranted such as computer programming skills or in physics, the skills of a mathematician able to compute the needed next step in a process. The processes that are involved must be of the simplest sort such that we all have evolved as a natural and necessarily in line with the capabilities that nature provides. Theorists imagine that no means of communication exists due to the empty vacuum presumption but once the vacuum is given the material needed to make the processes inevitable, then the evolution can possibly be understood.

Waves in the material vacuum are perhaps the force that drives all of our abilities and movements perhaps at the particle level. We might determine that matter has the attribute able to determine how fast the body can move in gravity but if all particles are surrounded by a gradient that allows objects into the surrounding envelope of particles then there need be no intelligence involved.

A common compression wave in the vacuum will have gradients between the variable intensity peaks and troughs able to grab and move any object, especially when acting on all particles in the object so that the gradient acts on all objects made of the same sized particles to multiply the attraction.

Likely, waves in vacuum can also be the electric current that enters into the brain through the facilities we already know, automatic wave interpreters that absorb the waves and feed them directly into the particle fields of brain. Networks of nerve fibers or waves must pass information around to every functionality in every structure of the brain where the necessary functionality is recognized and extracts the wave that belongs to it just as our networks function.

Our size is infinitely large attempting to understand the workings of an infinitely small set of mechanisms where we lack the ability to cheat our way into the system with microscopes or sharp pointed sensors in an attempt to pick the key for each functionality. This is the way our computer networks operate, perhaps unconsciously patterned after the way the brain works, much like AI systems may someday be able to build themselves using attributes that we accidentally provide them due to our ignorance about the systems that nature is providing.

A key is assigned by programmers that are placed at a designated location in every message that is sent. The intended recipients of messages compare their key with that of each message that is passed into the network held by each node in the network. In nature, the key may be the shape of the waves that form the message rather than a key so that when the message is for another node, when attempted to be read, a failure causes a rejection as a natural course while the wave continues onward.

The eyes pass a pattern wave that is different than the pattern of waves created by the ears due solely by mechanisms in the sensor and the way it is built. Smells are recognized by the wave structure. The skin has nerve structures that accept pressure sensations and the brain can create thoughts in a way that we can tell they are thoughts and not messages from outside. It is unlikely the key is a chemical molecule that must be passed around.

We think each sensor uses a hardwired connection to its specific lobe where it is processed in a way that we are likely to be able to see and that we can visually trace from the sensor to the lobe and then to the recipient of the message where it is acted upon. We can trace a visual message through the optic nerve into the brain where the connection is lost. We know that the gray matter of the brain is a logic network having various levels that perhaps search through a stored database of options.

Rather than the network choosing a correct response, every choice is acted upon and blindly sent to every possible response mechanism, perhaps to every muscle group and that is where the choice of response is tested for correctness. It may be that every possible choice of behavior is tested in the imagination system so that if we see an automobile, we try to get out of the way, fix it or whatever else that is possible.

If we act out all learned behaviors then the correct response will have been collected, along with all that are not correct. If at the same time the response is tested in the imagination system, a failure will be detected before the behavior is completed, saving us from foolish behaviors before they become apparently chosen. If no choice is made then we may not be as intelligent as we imagine.

If all the visual responses are stored and acted

upon, we will likely make the choice as researchers believe that the choice system that exists in the brain made the choice when all possible choices cannot be listed in the study. A choice is made in the researcher's brain and attributed to the test subject's brain. Each choice is an abstraction unto itself and the researcher will not list all that are available and in that way omit a choice that may be regarded as a side effect that is unimportant.

A wave structure is a three dimensional structure that will automatically replicate itself so that copies are washed across the brain, a process that is seen to happen as simple waves rather than waves containing information.   If every wave is an energy behavior, representing as a gradient that automatically chooses a behavioral response, then the proper choice will be made if sent everywhere possible so that inappropriate responses are tested and rejected. We may see it as an intelligent selection when no choice is made at all.

The information contained in a wave may be more than just wavelength though that is all we can detect, but each wave may be like a key where wavelength may be the first that is tested for a fit. Everywhere we go, we see objects too numerous to count and think that a hardwired response is represented by each of the dendrites and the paths that they allow. If each is a hardwired choice, not all can be acted upon without acting like a bumbling idiot, not a medical term, unless tried within the imagination system first with an imaginary set of results.

The choices that exist are formed in the memory systems where behaviors tried at an earlier time or that are read about in documentaries, or even in novels, where others have informally traced possible choices with the results that are tried with the elements that lead to success or failure. At a late stage in life, a large database of choices in all kinds of situations is stored but is unlikely stored as hard wired choices where each leads to a required choice, but if stored in a place where an infinite number of circumstances along with choices that are available, the choices may exist in the vacuum as stored waves that represent an infinite number of virtual realities.

The choices must be stored everywhere in every atom, if that is the mechanism, where the more places stored in the brain, entire scenarios may take no space at all but can be called upon using some mechanism that can recall memories where they are stored. The argument here must convincingly place the memories somewhere that can be accessed how they reach decisions in the logic system, complete with significant nuances. The system must be able to recognize the differences between abstraction and the complexities of reality.

While we tend to think of energy as a force able to move physical objects but if mechanisms that create the forces is waves able to overcome inertia of particles and more to be the momentum energy capturing the object to be moved in the gradients between the peaks and troughs. If waves are able to drive the human body to move in specific directions, the mantra that information is energy is in fact just that.

Light waves are also compression waves, a series of quantum sized waves that are emitted from a rotating or a source of alternating emission in directions along an antenna. The orbit model is theory which is the basis for electrons in orbit emitting them in series as the orbit is in progress. The electron is an atomistic particle, as are all particles, with an envelope of its own and it too may be absorbing the waves along with the proton envelope but in the model presented here, the electron is attached to a specific location on the surface of the atom and if the sinusoidal shape of the wave is from an orbiting object, the atom must have some freedom of movement and orbits are created to satisfy he behavioral findings of orbits, if the atom is forced to spin while emitting the waves, the theoretical model is satisfied in reality.

Emitted compression waves, like all waves, have momentum with no persistent core particle. The emission is an action that will have a reaction in the opposite direction forcing the electron to accelerate causing the atom to spin or increase the orbit allowing the sinusoidal structure.

Experiments establish that all particles of all sizes have a wave associated with it but no functionality is now being attributed to it, other than the duality of wave-particle behavior other than a peculiarity or an interesting discovery. Researchers still regard the vacuum as an empty space and the electromagnetic wave as a series of photons existing in a sinusoidal structure due to the orbits of emitting electrons.

The waves must be associated with the movement of particles, of all sizes. Here is no associated light and therefore not electromagnetic in nature. The wave must be of a sort that causes the inexplicable duality of particle aspect for theorists in the empty vacuum. Waves are used in physics in the wave functions in calculations for the electrons in orbit, for the count and structures thought to exist. The presumption of empty vacuum has been a fundamental part of theory for the past one hundred years and is an accepted fact though the presumption is not a provable condition and persists perhaps for the reason that the behaviors of theory may not be accurate if the vacuum is presumed otherwise.

One motivation for the undertaking herein is to show that particles presumed to be comprising the vacuum can exist only if the established behaviors are caused by the vacuum rather than creating a whole new theoretical base. This undertaking has first recognized theoretical findings and attempts to discover a mechanical causation that will produce the theoretical behavior.

An electron in orbit that is independent of the protons in the nucleus due to the waves that are emitted, the same behavior can result if the orbiting behavior is produced by a spinning atom or other mechanism described herein while the electrons are firmly attached to a proton. The attachment to the field of a proton allows for wave resources to be immediately available and a means for their storage as memories in the attached proton envelope with an infinite capacity using infinitely small particles of vacuum..

The orbiting electron behavior description of the atom is a model based on observable or detectable emissions. The orbiting model can produce a sinusoidal wave in a flat two dimensional plane which is supported by the experimental well known polarization of light representing oscillations of the emitter. Theoretical proofs include a model that can produce the behavior being described in the discovery but are known to be abstractions and not full representations of reality by there being no attempt to describe all elements that may be involved, discussed more completely in the section on ABSTRACTION herein.

The discovery of waves being attached to every moving particle is a very significant discovery that had been addressed when the quantum mechanical theory was being developed with mathematical representations of the finding but without the concept of material vacuum where momentum can be added to a moving particle as being argued here. The quantum energy is a reference to the photons carrying no rest mass but exhibiting momentum, the foundation for quantum mechanics.

Vacuum wave peaks are a moving compressed region in which the cores of vacuum particles are forced to be closer together. This description allows the momentum of quantum mechanics as well as the finding that photons have no rest mass, just as a wave peak will dissipate when coming to rest. Theorists first realized the quantum concept as a unit of energy and later referred to as a photon by Albert Einstein.

Movement of an object in empty vacuum theoretically will obey the laws of motion by not being subjected to any frictional forces. The vacuum particles being constructed essentially like the proton with its gravitational and magnetic fields, called the atomistic structure or archetype for all particles. The structure essentially eliminates all friction by the lubricating qualities of the surrounding small particles. It satisfies the theoretical gravity for all particles of mass while eliminating friction as in empty space.

Another law of motion is satisfied by the concept of the waves driving particles since the common compression wave is known to move through material mediums with the same continuous motion until meeting another force according to the first law of motion.

The a buildup of energy known as inertia to cause a mass to move is energy that can be explained by waves in terms of the buildup of a wave that begins the motion of inertia and further buildup is the construction of a wave that continues its momentum. Iit could be the phenomenon that gives all bodies in motion their momentum just as the Higgs Boson and other bosons , including the photon,   have wave properties and momentum.

The photon is argued here as quantum sized compression waves and only regarded as particles because of the empty vacuum presumption. The quality of having a quantity of momentum and no rest mass fits the wave property of the photon, a boson having the property that they can occupy the same space at the same time, also a property of waves.

The idea that all mass is driven by compression waves is not only somewhat like the Higgs Boson which is exactly like a wave by being the wave peak that looks like a particle that gives the property of mass to all moving particles. Mass is measured in terms of momentum, a numerical value, and the force or energy property of inertia, also a numerical value, the Higgs is also measured as a numerical value. Mass is measured by some procedure and not the matter it contains

There are theorists seeking to discover the Higgs Boson, and may well be looking for an ordinary compression wave. There can be no admission that for the past one hundred years of the presumption of empty vacuum has been an error in physics or the mechanism of the ordinary compression wave that cannot exist in empty vacuum. The argument being made here is that the ordinary compression wave is the mechanism that gives all particles their momentum, their mass. The claim there seems to be argued here, that the mechanism underlying all moving particles is the presence of a compression wave, including the bosons, being the wave itself..

Chemical energy for some molecules requiring heat to form will emit heat in the form of a heat wave when the bond is broken. The adenosine triphosphate (ATP) is an example that is the main energy source in biological systems. When energy is needed, the ATP breaks down to adenosine diphosphate (ADP) plus emission of heat energy, a heat wave.

Even the energy of electromagnetic waves (light) has been attributed to the photon and Einstein attributed the photon to a quantum of energy. It is being argued here that the photons in light are small quantum sized ordinary compression waves stuck together in the shape of a sinusoidal wave that have always been particles as an artifact of the empty vacuum. The photon in theory must be a particle since the only other choice is that it is an ordinary compression wave, an incomprehensible thought for a theorist bound to abide by the empty vacuum presumption.

MEMORY, MIND AND CONSCIOUSNESS

If memory is stored in the form that it is collected, in the form of an image or perhaps a conversation with a record of emotional responses, Then very little interpretation is required in passing the memory to the logic system of the gray matter where many possible answers to a single question can be selected and passed on to the brain through appropriate fibers or else as the selected set of waves broadcast. The selected wave information is sent to all the lobes of the brain where they may be selected if appropriate perhaps passing back a new question to be used for a new search.

While the forgoing operation may be the action that takes place but only as a single operation that is replicated in a huge number of the same operations taking place in parallel. Generally the search is to pass a past experience stored in memory that requires a response either as a modification of the returned memory and a message sent to a set of muscles or glands in the form of a command wave structure traveling through the fibers as a form of electrical current.

Theorists and physicists are looking in to the possibility of memory taking the form of pathways through the network of nerve fibers that can multiply the selections to take as a path or memory trace.

Several of the lobes have memory functions but only as a response to stimulation in patients that are awake who remarkably report a memory that can be reported, locating a specific location where a memory is a function of that location. How workers can replicate a wave that the brain generates is unlikely or be able to intercept a wave and interpret the data that it may contain so long as the presumption of empty vacuum persists.

We know that we can create speech as a conversation with ourselves as a normal property of the brain. It is likely that the memory system stores those conversations as thoughts that can be recalled by the logic system and announcement of discovery of it in some new situation. It would seem that storage even of thoughts would be an extravagant use of resources unless storage of thoughts and received data in unredacted form unless storage of memory uses no amount of resources in the vacuum of the brain though demonstrated as at expense of stored energy.

Thought waves will pass over the brain and meet one or many magnetic lines of force acting as an antenna that pass the waves to the proton envelope from which the antenna is attached. The wave that is passed to the proton envelope must undergo relativistic changes such as be flattened to infinitely thinness and placed on top of a stack of preceding experiences without occupying any space.

Memory is discussed in greater detail in the sections on MEMORY and that of RECALL. The section on CHEMISTRY covers how the elements are able to form bonds when exposed to a wave of energy or for another elemental atom the same energy can break a bond. What is not fully discussed is how molecules are passed around the body.

Today, only the movements of the molecules are being reported but nothing about what is causing it. Waves that are locally generated will likely be found that may lead to an electrical current or even breaking of a bond that emits a wave, either of which is controlled energy at work. It should be interesting to see what choices have been searched before a decision was made either in the brain or in a ganglion that sends a wave through a nerve fiber.

CHEMISTRY

The Hydrogen atom has a single proton and perhaps a neutron as its nucleus and a single electron in its magnetic gradient envelope, its field. A magnetic field is confined by its outer boundary of smallest vacuum particles giving the inner gradient its strength by having a confined gradient. All larger elemental atoms have closely bound protons comprising their nucleus and the same number of electrons and are all originally created within the extreme conditions inside a star.

There is nothing preventing Hydrogen atoms from being bound together in the nucleus to form any of the larger elemental atoms while their electrons are located in a fixed location relative to the nucleus above their protons in their magnetic fields. The evidence and benefits of this arrangement is argued herein.

The periodic table of the elements seeks to describe the elements in sequence according to the number of protons and electrons below and in the outer valence shell. Each shell has a set number of slots that can be filled before a new shell is formed creating an outer valence shell that is chemically active while causing the new inner shell to become inactive, as are all the inner shells.

The columns in each row of the table reflect the number of slots in the valence shell and below the valence shell that are filled and inactive. Some slots in the outer valence shell are not filled in the neutral state.. The filled slots begin at the left of the row of the element in the valence shell, so that those appearing in the left part of the row are metals with fewer filled valence slots and those in the right part of the row with few empty slots are the nonmetals.

The descriptions of the periodic tables refer to electrons being in shells generally referred to as being in orbits. It is just as likely that the shells are in the nucleus of the atom and the inactive inner shells are comprised of the protons with their electrons becoming inactive when covered by an outer shell. The magnetic fields of the outermost valence shell remains active as though it is a Hydrogen atom with its proton attached at creation of the element to the other protons in the nucleus by strong nuclear bonds. While firmly bound to the nucleus along with the other Hydrogen atoms, the magnetic envelope of the outer valence shell Hydrogen is free to grow in size by accepting wave peaks of both common waves, otherwise known as vacuum energy, and those quantum compression waves of the electromagnetic waves.

The magnetic field can grow in size as wave peaks of ordinary compression waves are accepted forming the magnetic lines of force while the electrons in the valence shell remain close to the body of the atom if involved with emission of eaves as opposed to antenna emissions of the proton's Faraday line of force. When electromagnetic waves are accepted, the atom may be forced to spin while emitting a sequence of quantum sized compressed waves to form another electromagnetic wave while spinning to cause the formation the sinusoidal shape of the electromagnetic wave. The same wave shape could be created by emission from an antenna. The emitted quantum sized waves all travel at the same rate, the velocity of light to maintain their structure, perhaps while attached as a single wave having more than one wave peak.

Because ordinary compression waves cannot exist in empty vacuum, the quantum sized waves are called photon particles in the theoretical empty vacuum. There are a number of particles, including photons that can occupy the same space at the same time as they intersect which is a wavelike characteristic. Photons have no rest mass but have momentum, both of which are wave characteristics.

The orbiting electron model of the atom depicts the nucleus as a cluster of protons forming a point from which a field is formed, both gravity and magnetic fields, while the electrons are theoretically able to find their own orbits. The protons in the nucleus must in reality each be able to affect the orbits of the their own individual electrons since without which they would likely form a single orbit in which they all fly but that is known not to be the case.

Another reality about the elements that fails to be explained by the theoretical model is how an electron in orbit is able to form a chemical bond. The element with slots in the valence shell is the model that chemists use in describing the ability of atoms to form bonds. Chemists may honor the prevailing view of the atom even though it may not conform to their working mode,. by finding that the electrons in orbit model allows understanding of the model supported in physics and theoretical physics where a great deal of information is presented in terms of that model while at the same time is disinformation about their own working mode.

The protons and their electrons, held in the proton envelope, is the description of the Hydrogen atom bound by a strong nuclear bond to others where the number of Hydrogen atoms defines the elements that are tabulated in the Periodic Table of the Elements. The Hydrogen atoms are held in the nucleus in shells rather than the free electrons in orbit as the Table describes as the electrons alone in shells that are represented in the Table by the row number or columns that represent groups having similar functions. Herein, electrons are in shells with their protons.

The Hydrogen atoms in the lower shells become inactive by being covered by the outer layers or shells leaving the outer shell, the valence shell, to remain active as Hydrogen atoms whether or not the protons are accompanied by inactive neutrons that increase the weight and gravity, being incorporated in a higher elemental atom, but is not counted or affect atomic number of the element.

Using the Periodic Table of the Elements, the location of the element in the table is significant in how that particular element's chemistry will be like. If the element is listed in the lower rows, they are lighter in weight and in the atomic number, the number of protons in the atom. If the element of interest can be found in a row, the position in the row will reflect the chemical activity of the element.

MEMORY, MIND AND CONSCIOUSNESS

The smaller elements are below a selected element to be analyzed and to the left in the row in which it exists. By counting the elements that are smaller the inner nature of the selected element will be better understood. If it exists near the far left end of its row then it is likely to behave as a metal with one or a few isolated electrons with a number of empty slots to the right of its location. The metals can react to form bonds with the nonmetals that are to the right having partially filled slots with a few empty slots.

Biologists and particularly histologists studying the tissue types, biochemists and physiologists seek to understand the functionality of tissues. The primary focus on brain function is the contacts that are made between the nerve cells and the methods of passing information from one cell to another, where receptors are the short but numerous dendrites. Information is passed down the long fiber of the cell, the axon, after receiving it at the tips of the dendrites where the function of the synapses are studied..

Long axons are insulated by a lining of myelin sheath cells, except when within the brain. Axons within the spinal cord are most likely disqualified due to the insulation from being antenna but when within the brain will likely be able to capture the brainwaves that seem to flood the brain area. At the ends of the axons are the axon terminals of more dendrites and the synapse that pass information to the dendrites of the next nerve cell in line.

The nerves exiting the brain by means of the spinal cord reaching the various parts of the body, very complete instructions are sent to the mobile parts such as the fingers, arms and legs and sensations are received and returned through other nerve fibers that are processes by the networks and structures within the brain that serve the nerves entering and leaving the brain.

The axons within the brain are not protected by the insulation myelin sheaths possibly allowing them to receive impulses in the form of waves which is the main concern here since waves are the focus of this book. Waves are passed from the exterior into the nervous system acting as electricity which can be detected using EEG scans of the brain. The electricity generated by the eyes, ears and so on are passed into the brain by means of nerve fibers to the parts of the brain that service the various parts of the body able to read these weak signals and possibly amplify them..

Electrical waves may be strengthened by high energy molecules containing bonds that break to emit stronger waves, typical are molecules, the adenosine triphosphate

(ATP) bonds known in biochemistry to drive neural impulses which yield energy, as compression waves, through hydrolysis, the addition of water, to lose a phosphate to produce ADP, a double phosphate molecule. Literature only refers to the process as a source of energy without describing the nature, most likely as heat.

These are possibly the sources of the many waves that are detected by the EEG scans that can only detect the wavelengths and strengths. A weak wave may be boosted by the ATP to ADP conversion or a super fast high energy wave produced from a quantum entangled channel may serve to break loose memory structures in the proton envelopes, a hypothesis based on material vacuum that may have been inexplicable in sciences due to the presumption of empty vacuum.

Very large waves are possible, contrary to quantum mechanics, arising as theories on studies of light where the quantum waves, argued herein, are regarded as photon particles, a symptom growing out of the empty vacuum presumption. Waves in the vacuum arriving at the sensory nodes of neurons require no conversion to electrical impulses to be sent as electrical pulses since electric current is very likely movement of vacuum waves within a circuit.

DARK MATTER MECHANICS

Rather than specific atoms storing waves as memories of wave based activity, they may as well be sent to all the atoms in the brain since, as analyzed herein, they occupy no space whatsoever. A wave that leaves out certain facts of reality as stored in reality databases are interpreted as questions and complete confirmation of facts are added to the databases, also stored as memories in the same atoms in the brain, very likely the dendrites of the logic systems.

Analysis of this concept is set out in the sections on INFINITY, VACUUM and ATOMS. The protons of the Hydrogen structures in the strong magnetic fields can behave as gravity fields of large celestial bodies that are analyzed in regard to Einstein's theories of relativity and proven behavior as modified herein and explained as phenomena of the material vacuum. As a compression wave passes deeper into a gradient, some of the particles will gain in mass and be buoyantly removed from the wave and the remainder will flatten and the speed will begin to be reduced.

All permanent atoms in the brain during brain growth are quantum entangled able to send waves in a much different inertial frame of very small vacuum particles. The spaces between memory waves will separate, reversing the previous effects of relativity in the process of storage. These connections are not at all conceivable to theorists, where mechanisms cannot exist in empty vacuum. These are inflated by smaller particles allowing them to rise into the Faraday tubes as antenna for access and emission.

The atoms themselves may not have logic mechanisms, though that is not at all certain, but the brain provides the logic for assessing what parts of the body should be involved in resolving questions or reacting to facts that are threatening. Learned behaviors at the far ends of neurons are processed by ganglia in the spinal cord in the same way that the brain processes them to some extent. The ganglion's responses are supervised by the brain by much slower processes even though sent to and from the brain as waves or electrical impulses that are processed as waves.

A record of all activity and sensed behaviors incurred as a constant record regardless of the meanings but when there is a period of sleep or isolation, the brain will pull out the time periods in a last in first out process as far back in time as required or that is allowed by other brain activity. Sleep allows the past to be analyzed quietly or as active dreams, messaging the memories as a whole or as pieces able to construct fantasies that are analyzed for logicality though, obviously, the same can occur during waking hours.

There are spaces between nerves at the synapses which have been analyzed in terms of the chemical exchanges that are made, emitted by one end and collected at the end of another nerve. These may contain necessary material for maintenance of the nerve tissues but should not be thought of as passing information which is done through waves that contain all the information and more that is needed for the needed mental processes.

The correlation of waves and electricity is so efficient that it cannot be ignored, though inconceivable by theorists who are bound by the presumption of empty vacuum. As for belief systems that are contrary to the facts held in the data of the brain, they may come from very old memories when facts were very limited. If one grows up in an environment of old memories, as in family belief systems, even new memories will be afflicted with missteps.

Common belief regarding waves in molecular mediums that the molecules move closer to each other in wave peaks in transporting the momentum of the wave. While that may be the case, it is likely the vacuum waves that cause molecules to move which find their way into the brain. While the concepts being discussed herein are original without footnotes to sources because there are no sources because the activity described herein are activities that take place in the vacuum which is naturally not discussed in theoretical literature because of the presumption of empty vacuum and should be viewed by the reader as such.

Theorists avoid discussion of the role that vacuum plays even though it is obviously vacuum behavior. When that occurs, the behavior is described without any discussion of causation, unless as an aside, since theory is devoted to describing behavior and how it relates to other behavior allowing perpetuation of the empty vacuum presumption.

The vacuum behavior being described here are not entirely without proof partly because the behavior is already established in theoretical physics or by other theoretical professionals but without addressing any possible mechanisms or mechanical causation.

The conclusions set out herein are based on ground up mechanical theory beginning with the type of particles that must exist in the vacuum to allow the properties that have been observed in the vacuum. There cannot be friction due to the laws of motion that are based on empty vacuum where friction cannot exist but empty vacuum would collapse with the slightest pressures of surrounding matter but if particles are all surrounded by vacuum gradients with no empty space whatsoever, the small particles lubricate movement of their particles and also those of larger particles.

The particles of vacuum must also be surrounded by a relative vacuum of their own and the gradients that prevent collapse of the vacuum and further lubricate movement. Earlier, materials discussed here were created in a set of research notes as the concepts were advanced where some failed to meet the needs of reality. Publications of the ideas set out herein are the result of the many rewrites and additions to the notes.

The project began with seeking to understand the ideas of Einstein in his theories of relativity and adding matter to the vacuum brought all the concepts in line with a reality not just being described as behavior but as causation. The fact that particles increase in mass with acceleration raises the question of where the extra matter comes from and by adding matter from the vacuum is a reasonable resource for the added matter and explaining the length contraction..

The concept of functional Hydrogen added to the nucleus was conceived as a means for satisfying the needs of chemistry allowing the outer valence shell to exist as a pattern on the surface of the atom. Chemistry already views the atom as having a valence shell having filled and vacant slots for electrons. A filled slot of a metal can provide an electron to an empty slot of a nonmetal in forming a bond where electrons alongside the slot help in forming the bond.

The orbiting electron model seems not to be conceived to allow the behavior while only able to account for effects of electromagnetic waves in terms of allocation of energy stored in changes in orbiting electron radius. What happens after a bond is formed to the orbits or how orbits can cause a bond to form is one of many weaknesses in the orbiting electron model if regarded as a complete description of the atom. As an abstraction, the orbiting electron model has its benefits in precision of energy allocation as driven by waves using the wave function of the more modern model.

Single Hydrogen holding its electron in the magnetic envelope will accept waves due to the momentum of the vacuum particles closest to the outer membrane forced forward against the envelope as a peak of the wave. The vacuum in the peak is more dense then the vacuum in the surrounding regions due to the particles in the peak being forced closer together. This density will cause the wave to enter and be drawn closer to the proton in the magnetic gradient.

These are comprised of the larger core particles pushed together adding to the momentum that the peak carries that buoyantly pushes the electron away from the proton in conformity with the quantum mechanics placing the electron in a higher energy state by the expansion of the envelope, theoretically in an orbital. The electron is also an atomistic particle with a magnetic field of its own allowing it to respond by emission of the electromagnetic wave to reduce its volume which in turn allows it to buoyantly move to a lower position, again, conforming to the quantum mechanical model. Possibly more realistic is emission from the Faraday tubes responding to the pressure from inside envelope extending and reducing the length in response.

At the same time, the magnetic gradient of the proton envelope will become enlarged or more compressed extending or strengthening the magnetic lines of force, the Faraday tubes, now described in accordance to the mathematical of theory as a field density rather than lines of force as originally described by Faraday.

These lines of force or fields are enhanced during

the generation of electricity, charging a closed circuit that cuts across the fields of a magnet. The magnet can be enhanced by a wrap or coil of another current carrying circuit generally around a permanent magnet but also a simple bar or even an empty space. The charging circuit will have increased potential or current as it cuts across the lines of force. A battery, of course, will also increase the potential of a circuit.

Theory describes electric current as electrons moving down the circuit but, as with photons, a compression wave has many of the characteristics of a particle which is more likely being mistaken as electrons in support and to perpetuate the empty vacuum presumption by assigning current to known particles rather than a behavior of matter that is not supposed to be present. Photons as current may be a better particle than electrons as waves of vacuum.

Proton envelopes stretch by influx of vacuum waves allowing electrons to have the appearance of freedom. Electric current exists without damage to the metal atoms of circuitry as would be expected by removal of electrons. Compression waves will behave as electrons but will have temporary mass that is maintained in high potential, voltage.

A moving charging circuit is forced across a

magnetic field allowing the vacuum matter to be forced into the circuit as potential or current. The proton envelopes will extend as an enhanced magnetic field that feeds compressed waves of electricity into the charging circuit that is forced into the charging circuit most likely due to its own motion across the magnetic gradient in a generating station though current from batteries do the same thing.

These lines do not directly affect the location of the electron which remains relatively close to the proton, at a distance that is in accordance with the quantum mechanical orbital radius and detected as current in the empty vacuum

MISCELLANEA

Physics, has often repeated the mantra referencing "the mechanical universe" and in serving that declaration it is the science of recording and measuring observable behavior with particular attention to measuring the cause and effect relationships when possible when addressing the issue of causation. Much has been written on the philosophy of the issue, whether the cause must precede the effect of the effect or how directly the cause must be. Many have not abandoned the notion of cause and effect in physics saying that every effect that is observed in physics, there is an implied cause, though it may not be immediately obvious.

Others argue that the notion of causation is a concept of the past and is no longer a physical reality or at least in the physics and theoretical undertaking of these two sciences. In the past, some have observed that we should look into the vacuum where virtually all causation is occurring but that it cannot be directly verified through current means using the scientific method.

While it may be that the scientific method as used today is not able to verify the behavior that is occurring in the vacuum, not even if its obviousness is present for all to see. Some might argue that the indirect and circumstantial evidence to prove a behavior in the vacuum or even to establish that it is a medium and not empty space, is to revert back to the past where it was obvious that the world is flat or that the atmosphere is empty space. It was the same kind of evidence that first established that the earth is round. The molecules in air have never been observed but it was use of the scientific method that established the genes in plants or that molecules exist in air.

The issue is not that accepting indirect or circumstantial evidence of what is occurring in the vacuum but whether the measurements and relationships that are being derived in physics is now devoid of possible causation which is being supplied here through reliable methods if not use of the experimental methods of the science. The measurements that are being taken in physics and satisfaction with behavior in theory is of value in engineering settings but fails to be true science due to omission of any cause and effect determinations.

MEMORY, MIND AND CONSCIOUSNESS

Measurements and descriptions of behavior in the field of unobservable behavior that are essentially mathematically derived from findings in physics, now known as theoretical physics, is most useful and has opened many doors in technology, especially in electronic devices, where photographic images of electrical circuits and logic are used by photographically zooming out to create ever smaller and more intricate features that are created in very large images. It seems that we are perhaps reaching the limits of how images of light can be used in further miniaturization that must be overcome before even smaller and more circuitry can be added to a device.

An example of miniaturization that usually does not come to mind is that of holographic images that present themselves as three dimensional by means of the entire image being held on every grain of the photograph. They are not ordinary images but rather are taken in a laser light field. It is not that we fully understand how the process works or the mechanism that is involved to make the effect come about but that we can describe the behavior and the techniques to make it come about which may be enough to "fully understand" holography.

The claim is being made here that certain physical structures that are described here and in the previous volume in the series "Dark Matter Mechanics: Introduction to a Science of Vacuum" is derived not from mathematical computations of theoretical physics but that the mathematics has already been done but that the models used to illustrate the properties being claimed to be discoveries are not, nor were they ever, intended to be a representation of reality but rather of the mathematics and abstractions of behavior.

It is further claimed here that theories leave out much that is being claimed here to be very important as the mechanisms of the behavior being described by theorists. This is known to be the process of abstraction where a feature is focused upon by omitting much of the unrelated material that could be proven to be present if that were the point of the discovery.

This technique of proof solely using mathematics alone can be attributed largely to Prof. Einstein and his theoretical approach to discovery. Though he is known for being a physicist, his most famous discoveries were in mathematics where he was able to use experimental discoveries, such as the increases in mass of a particle when accelerated or the limitations of the speed of light to falsify the previous concepts of presumed instantaneous transmission of an image not dependent on the speed of light to convey information.

While some may disagree, much of his work was using techniques in mathematical extrapolation and extension of known reality that had not been addressed in theories. There were others seeking to reach many of the same conclusions he reached using properties of aether, a material that was generally held to be present in the vacuum but failed to beat Einstein in publishing their results to be largely dismissed today as not significant or not to be found today.

The arguments made in this text are discussed in great mechanical detail involving the nature and form that vacuum must have to allow the fields to exist and the total lack of friction that allows the laws of motion to take place. The difference between the aether of the past and the vacuum being presented here is the great variety of sizes of particles necessary for the field structures to exist and frictionless behavior to exist where ever smaller particles in structures provide lubrication. Aether was theoretically a standing gas and was responsible for the luminiferous aether able to transmit the light waves only.

The largest particles of vacuum must be extremely small, so small that physicists have been able to presume their nonexistence over the past century without much argument since whenever the appropriate assignment to behavior should be to the vacuum, it went to detectable particles that are associated with the vacuum in question. It is said that particles have fields rather than the fields that clearly exist as the vacuum. A large problem with empty space existing between the particles and inside the parts of the atoms is that they should quickly close and cease being empty space. The structures described herein prevents any empty space whatsoever from occurring.

Devising vacuum that holds the particles apart by having no empty space and yet allows the particles to slide past each other as in a liquid could be regarded as a discovery in itself. However, the discovery requires a virtually infinite size range of particles in a mathematical convention that is more than just annoyed by the concept of infinity, even though regularly used in mathematical proofs and in the calculus and analytical geometry, while at the same time ruling that an infinite result is an error or a NaN.

The concept of proton envelopes is introduced as a physical property of Hydrogen atoms and the nuclear particles of the atom where there are as many proton envelopes containing an electron as there are protons in the nucleus forming the shells now being attributed to electrons in their orbits. For another thing, electrons are firmly held in the proton envelopes and only in orbit if the entire atom is allowed or caused to spin. The Faraday tubes are a likely candidate for many functions though doubt of their existence exists much like doubt regarding vacuum.

By presuming the vacuum is a material substance, it is possible to find in the vacuum that ordinary waves can and do exist. The "ordinary" or "common" waves are those that contain particles that can be drawn closer together as the wave peak and where wavelengths are the distance from one compression to the next rather than from one deviation from the zero line to the next in a sinusoidal shape of connected quantum waves in the electromagnetic wave.

Theorists working under the impression that vacuum is empty space cannot find that ordinary waves can exist and must find a carrier for much of the properties that are being detected, like photons as quantum waves. The infinite particle sizes comprising vacuum should allow it to be called an infinite space and in an infinite space, where infinitely small structures can exist. As in holograms, it should be possible for entire images, even an infinite number of entire images to be held in a single quantum photon or common wave peak.

While that is not exactly what is needed to form an

opinion of how vacuum is used in the brain for transmission of information, there are many brainwaves being detected inside the bony skull containing the brain that are determined to have frequencies that differ. These are known from which diagnosis of temperament and mental health are said to be possible.

These waves have been determined to not contain information but that cannot be a conclusive determination since we lack the ability to make that determination. These waves are apparently viewed as the same as light or electromagnet since they are being detected using conventional means. Other types of waves may be possible such as those that drive particles that may be unknown outside of the brain or are those that look like electrons in an electrical circuit but are not electrons existing in the cerebrospinal fluid surrounding all CORTEX regions and is likely the main means of communication.

Regarding visual sensory information as light, there is likely a misunderstanding regarding light as visual information used by the brain. They are not particles flying directly in straight lines from the source to the sensory organ that detects it. Light emissions are spherical in shape and the particle of light is more likely due to the size of the orifice that detects a part of the sphere. A photon that is seen as a particle is a piece of continuous spherical waves stacked one on top of the other. It is rather obvious that an object continuously emitting light in spherical waves, the first will be a larger sphere that reaches the eye before any of those that have yet to reach the eye. It has to be this way for an image to be shared among all those looking at the image. Between the emitter and the receiver, there are continuously growing sets of spheres.

By the time a bit of light reaches the sensory organ, the spheres have begun to be extensively stacked so that a piece of the sphere will contain many stacked images with the first emission being the outermost concentric layer that may be too far apart that a simple form of compression would be simply to cause the layers to rest closer together when stored. While the source continues to emit light in concentric layers that seem to be stacked layers at the point being perceived, saving the brain from creating time dependent overlays of images, it being a physical property of light taking place before the image ever reaches the observer.

It is easy to say that the brain remembers images, or for that matter, sees images. It should go without saying that the brain does have the facility for seeing images and it must be that facility being used both for vision and inner vision when recalling a visual event. That remembering an image is not quite as vivid as when first seen in present time, some loss in the images is perhaps due to compression effects.

While the literature may not describe waves passing over the CORTEX structures of gray matter that can be read using EEG equipment, it seems logical that every sensation and sensory reception must pass over the layers of gray matter for logic assessment before passing any further into or out of the brain. The waves are likely carried in the cerebrospinal fluid which is directly in touch with the gray matter.

A sort of wave cycle for sensory receptor waves, perhaps neatly put together for processing first in the specific parts of the brain dedicated for its type of input and a set of waves emitted with an identifier of the type of wave. They are then passed over the carpet of dendrites of the gray matter, generally as brainwaves containing information about what was detected, passed through the layers of gray matter for logic assessment and from there to the nerves of the body as needed through the BRAINSTEM. The CORTEX is divided generally into various functionalities as set out in the ANATOMY section of the text so that if the entire

CORTEX also processes the waves, the essential parts of focus will be adequately taken care of in any case.

The cranial nerves are input and output and enter the brain at the bottom of the brain into specialized parts of the brain where first processed before being passed over the gray matter logic for processing and coordination with other current inputs. The neural network designs for computer processing generally are explained as every entry node is linked to every node in the next layer and a comparison value of identity is placed to compete for the next level to allow a thorough analysis and elimination of the weakest links. A hardwired connection of the near infinite items to be compared is not likely if what amounts to broadcast waves will do the same thing.

In other words, very much of brain linkages are probably broadcast waves where identifiers are included in the wave to allow receptors to determine if relevant information is in the wave needing attention, much like some local computer networks work or Wi-Fi emissions work. Relevance could be a repetitious and highly automatic run through the logic system to allow association of various different sources of information as wave content. A reproduction of an entire past experience complete with visual, sound and other senses all are stored and brought to the front where dated experiences are remembered.

The brainwaves that are being intercepted by EEG equipment are measured in wavelengths and if episodes of an experience are stored in the quantum waves of electromagnetic waves, the longer wavelengths are likely to be more complete episodes by having more of the quantum wave elements and shorter wavelength waves are likely more immediate sensory receptions by having fewer quantum elements. The waves can have a mixture of both long and short wavelengths as demonstrated using the mathematical technique of Fourier analysis to count each contained wavelength.

There can be no causes that can be validated unless the presumption of empty vacuum is abandoned. Even then, this attempt at discovery of causation as a mechanical means herein cannot be validated with certainty using current technology. It is circumstantial evidence used here that should be a valid means of discovery without being accused of abandoning the scientific method. We can each assess the functionality of the brain for ourselves knowing that mechanisms must be at work. The principle of causation is the relationship between two events where one must precede the other and is a consequence of the other. Entanglement is a means of passing information faster than electrical means, the speed of light. Some have argued that if the principle of cause and effect is violated, it perhaps may cause the end the world as we know it. Entanglement does not change the order of the original events.

It is not that the principle of causality has been abandoned but is now implicitly present with every change that occurs as an honorarium or implicit thought toward a cause and effect truism. Quantum entanglement was possibly the break between local causation and theory by calling it spooky action at a distance by Einstein, acknowledging its existence and experimental evidence has established that entangled information is faster than ordinary perception giving a glimpse into the immediate future as an earlier glimpse of the past. The path to understanding is to apply the laws of physics rather than abandoning them even though the applied mathematics, an entirely different field of study, must generally be satisfied. Entanglement allows learning about an event occurring in the past more quickly, not before it happens but faster than ordinary means of transmission. The process therefore does not defeat the concept of causality where the principle of causation requires that causes must precede the effects.

DARK MATTER MECHANICS

Some effects are studied without having the ability to determine causation leaving the only choice to measure the effects only. Physics records descriptions of effects but not causation relationships by reducing them to mathematical expressions but mathematics has no way to express causation. There is a fundamental difference by sequencing of events relating two different events, not just restating one differently as in the preferred principle of action reaction relationships.

Chemistry has a way to express cause and effect by using a timeline arrow to point the direction of causality. While a reaction will only occur among an expected percentage of reactions, it does point the direction of the changes that do occur. There are other factors that occur after the arrow but mixing the reactants as shown on the left is the intentional causal event.

In the text, something or many things can cause a wave to be generated but the immediate cause of the effect is the wave itself. What causes the wave could be the elastic nature of the gradient structures. If a gradient moves in the vacuum causing the gradient to deform, it will then reform causing the domino effect that should be generic enough to be a natural cause for creating a wave.

MEMORY, MIND AND CONSCIOUSNESS

Mass is a measurement of behavior but some experts taught that it measures the amount of matter in the body of mass. To determine the mass, a measured energy is applied to the mass until movement of the mass is observed as the measure of inertia that exists in the mass. What causes the energy that overcomes the inertia of the mass, standard techniques are applied using published standards.

Of course, energy is movement itself as acceleration of a mass over a distance and has little if any other meaning other than potential. Force is often used to refer to causation or work, but for every force that is applied, as argued herein, a wave with a gradient that can either capture the mass or not, and if not, a greater wave must be created if movement is to be achieved, a process that may qualify as the energy of inertia and momentum .

Waves contain gradients between the peaks and troughs over the normal density of the vacuum. The gradient can cause movement by means of buoyancy principles where an unequal pressure against one side of a body of mass will cause it to move. There is experimental evidence that for every moving particle of whatever size, an associated wave is present argued herein to be the energy that causes the movement provided the vacuum is as discussed herein.

DARK MATTER MECHANICS

Mechanics may have been abandoned as a reality in favor of a philosophy that argues that if every behavior has a causation that prevents any other behavior, it represents fatalism or loss of free will. The logic system avoids that result by somehow leaving choice in behavior based on past outcomes by examining the past, some of the stored memories, but none will be found to be exactly controlling though having elements that are significant. Of course, exact replicas occurring too often will be chosen, but the ability to err is likely the ability to chose since correct behavior cannot be agreed upon by all.

For some relationships, there is no obvious observable causation, not the usual obviousness of physics by not being observable, though there are observable effects such as gravity and magnetic fields and also electricity where using the theories and models of theoretical physics provides very little help. These variables can be set equal to itself by another name and preceded by a negative sign, where conveniently, that name is invariably energy, which itself is a behavior.

This equality and reference to an effect leaves the false impression that energy is the causation for the behavior where in effect, the expression is generally just another definition for the name on the other side of the equation sign which is in no way the causation of the measured effect.

The result of the forgoing is that both of these sciences are studies in behavior only, which is a very useful ambition but has given the impression that knowing measurements of a behavior is full understanding of the behavior. This is the obvious influence of theoretical physics or otherwise known as mathematical physics, a field of applied mathematics using the mathematically expressed findings of physics, where physicists very carefully determine factual findings, albeit, usually facts regarding relationships.

Energy equals mass times the velocity of light squared is Einstein's famous equation for energy where the equation variables can be set to the remainder of the equation under rules of mathematics. The velocity of light is not always comparable to the speed in a different inertial frame, according to Einstein where the difference, according to him, is the velocity of the inertial frame that changes the amount of matter of objects in the inertial frame including, argued here, the matter in the vacuum.

Physicists and theorists know a great deal about the properties of vacuum though using a workaround to avoid attributing these properties to vacuum itself but rather to an object that is easily associated with the property such as gravity, magnetic fields of the object or electricity where the electrical current is likely not the theoretical electrons but rather waves in the vacuum medium of the material of the circuit.

The brain is an object that is constructed according to the DNA of the owner with generally the same shape and properties among all the owners whose brains can or have been examined, particularly, the anatomy and histology. It could be said that the physiology of the brain is also fairly well understood but for the most fundamentals regarding it as the reservoir of memory, mind and consciousness, now being deemed attributes of nature that simply cannot and will never be understood other than how it affects the owner's behavior.

What we do know is basically the same as for physics, but for the fact of causation, and what effects that are known, they are generally subconscious and only sparingly revealed. As for physics and theoretical physics, tact has been taken that is well understood as valid evidence of an underlying truth that is unrevealed as an objective truth. When the experts determine that a behavior repeatedly occurs precisely in the same way and under precisely the same conditions, in empty space, guided and perpetuated by an original source of energy, there must be an underlying truth that is being completely overlooked.

Where physics is perhaps the simplest of the sciences, the brain is perhaps the most complex, but like physics, the apparent complexity that is due to inexplicable phenomena, but once the underlying truth about the phenomenon is known, the blinders are pulled away and understanding is revealed. The simplest discoveries may be a foundation for explaining some of the most persistent hidden and misunderstood truths, such as the discovery that a moving particle is always accompanied by a wave no matter the size of the particle. In a science that refuses to admit the presence of matter in the vacuum, the discovery of an unexpected wave must be a stunning fact.

The natural, though circumstantial, conclusion that all movement is actually caused by an associated wave may seem like a trivial discovery, but that it finally is a fundamental mechanical causation for the much overused variable, that of energy as inertia and momentum.

We regularly see overwhelming data for the count of brain cells and their dendrite extensions providing a multiplier thereof for the number of connections that occur within the brain. While this observation may be circumstantial evidence of something about the brain, unless we can determine the meaning of the dendrites and their connections, the circumstances of their count has little meaning without discovery of the mechanisms involved by calling on all the scientific knowledge to help explain the mechanisms to the extent that they may be available.

Brain scientists or scientists in general, see in their imagination, electrons traversing through the nerve axons and through selected dendrites as electrical current transmitting pulses that trigger a behavior and back again through sensory dendrites and axons as confirmation of the expected behavior.

Whether it is electrons or waves in the vacuum, as argued herein, the pulse must contain information other than a simple presence. More likely, an information wave will be sent to a number of receptors that are able to distinguish its identity in the wave or that of another and react accordingly, but science has yet to acknowledge the existence of vacuum or vacuum waves so that electrons have been selected for the task.

Scientists are guided by physics and theoretical physics and their findings and presumptions. The empty vacuum presumption leads them to believe that a particle must be moving through the circuit as electrical current. Photons might have been a better choice as information carrying particles which are more likely to be waves, leaving no residue of particles if a circuit is unexpectedly broken.

The empty vacuum presumption resulting in an inability for waves to be present, notwithstanding the ever presence of brainwaves, compels brain scientists to seek hardwired connections or paths of electrical means of communication as the model for memory. Physics has become a science of observable behavior so that they search for the objects that can be observed and can be confirmed as having existence as a matter of fact and attribute them with the missing needs or explanations that are being sought.

A simple glance at the great detail of what we see, hear, taste, smell, feel and other sensations around us that we are constantly being subjected to, whether we take notice of everything or not, it is difficult to believe that there might be enough pathways available to complete the task, though a pathway may be a string of bits or a path to a location where a set of images may be stored. With all the sensations that are constantly flowing into the brain and subject to recall at any moment, the task seems enormous.

DARK MATTER MECHANICS

As for vision, if we see entire images, whether or not we remember them in great detail, from which we can at any time extract detail, a great many details and connections would be required, more than the brain could ever handle without replacing some from time to time, and there is little evidence that memories are lost by acquiring new ones.

The brain operates on a scale that can be imagined that allows a great many operations per second that all operate at once, allowing the brain to process information, as we all know, at a rate that cannot be calculated with the end result being movement of a muscle along with all the realizations that the brain must accompany every movement of every muscle.

Consciousness means that the sensory receptors are capturing waves in the atmosphere or detecting familiar chemical attributes like taste, smell and feel as sensations that only the owner can describe using memory of the events of the past and many of the details that accompanied those memories of sensations. It is easy to imagine that a part of the brain is responsible for the visual senses operating to recall similar visuals from the past as a vague set of images or as a different quality, as knowledge or as recognition of a part of an event of the past.

MEMORY, MIND AND CONSCIOUSNESS

The process may be a collection of bits that each must be addressed when recalling an image, much like a computer sending an image a line at a time. The more modern computers are able to process millions of bits per second, allowing us to believe that it is a relatively simple process that the brain might easily replicate, but the computer does not think and only has very few imputes to process whereas the brain has many.

Entire images used as the objects of memory, the number of images used in this way greatly reduce the quantity of data that may need to be stored. On the other hand, in this and the previous volume, the fact that size in this universe is almost inconsequential if there is an infinite range of sizes in the two directions of the large and small of infinity. The use of connections in the brain, as large and many as there are, compared to infinitely many of infinitely small matter, the number of connections are almost measly.

Biochemistry has also been investigated for the reservoir of memories where new molecules or connections within molecules are a pathway for memory. The contradiction of biochemistry like nerve connections is that a new memory requires sacrificing the old. There is no evidence in literature or in personal experience that memories must be sacrificed in order to acquire new memories of experiences.

It is apparent that memories take up little if any space in the brain that would cause a limitation of what can be retained as memories, mind or consciousness. Computer sciences are constantly reducing the size of devises being used in computers but never yet reduced to the size of an atom but rather the simplest line is made of many atoms in a line in a printed circuit.

We have yet to produce a device able to offer unlimited memory but evolution has apparently taken advantage of the raw material to which it has access of which we have little confirmable knowledge.

The brain is a system that scientists, of course try to use what is known to explain the brain, and are constantly finding new inventions regarding the subject they are studying.   Scientists   are   at   a   distinct disadvantage by being subjected to the required use of mathematics, for one thing, because it among other concepts are   abstractions, omitting mechanisms by requiring only descriptions of behavior which is nothing more than abstractions.   The attempt here is to take advantage of the freedom to investigate to the fullest a substance that has yet to be addressed and thereby avoiding contradiction of any concepts already in the literature if set out herein.

MEMORY, MIND AND CONSCIOUSNESS

There are no words in theoretical physics that address causation which was once the substance of physics. Some would argue that at least references to the energy in physics causes a behavior. Not so. Energy is defined as mass and acceleration, or Einstein's velocity squared, but neither acceleration nor mass can cause its own behavior. Energy is a word that describes behavior when movement is observed and the same is true of force. Force is likewise a behavior acting in the same way as energy, if a movement is observed then it can be said that force is present.

This is not an empty argument since theorists agree that causation is not and cannot possibly be included in any accepted theory. Force and energy may be conditions precedent or necessary conditions but are not a primary cause, albeit, not a cause at all. Einstein's theories contained evidence that we know very little of our reality.

The aether was abandoned after a certain expected property was not found in the Michelson-Morley experiments, when the aether wind was not detected that was thought should have affected the speed of light, but it did not. The experiment did not measure velocity of the aether which would change the sizes of vacuum particles which would have affected the speed of light but it was the velocity of every part of the instrument of measure, not the aether itself. Only change from one inertial frame to another where one had undergone a process that changes sizes of vacuum particles as energy needed to move the particles that are forming as waves. So far as we know, that can only be achieved through acceleration but the aether was at all times regarded as a standing gas through which absolute measures were to be determined.

Acceleration is able to change the mass of particles and therefore the content of the nonempty vacuum. The Michelson-Morley experiments was not evidence that would confirm or deny the presence of a vacuum medium, nor was it a teaching moment but without some knowledge of what could cause a change in the velocity of light, the concept of the aether wind was a mere shot in the dark.

The idea that gravity would cause the same effects as the acceleration of an inertial frame, conceived by Einstein by the mathematics of gravity and acceleration being the same could not give him the proof of a physical reality that actually does exist. He used the astronomical evidence that light bends around a gravitating body compared to light traveling in a straight line being the shortest distance, maybe. Curvature of changes in density of vacuum was what he noticed. It was long after publication of his theories that he admitted that he thought vacuum was a substance.

A body collects around it the largest particles in the surrounding vacuum to create its gradient in the vacuum. Therefore, gravity effectively creates change in the inertial frame at one location within the gradient compared to another within it or to anywhere that is outside of it. He had been influenced by the elimination of vacuum as a variable by the empty vacuum presumption but he had to know, consciously or unconsciously, that the differences in inertial frames are the vacuum within it. Once a causation is known, it is easy to describe behavior within one compared to another using mathematics, even though he was unable.

The experimental discovery of changes in mass of an accelerated body was the basis of most of Einstein's theories of relativity though he addressed it as a cause very seldom, if at all, or modern literatures about his theories have omitted that as a consideration in order to maintain the illusion of the empty vacuum. Einstein's theory that energy equals mass times the speed of light squared was derived mathematically by extrapolation of the fact of the change of mass through acceleration but there is nothing in that equation predicting that mass increases to infinity as would be required for his theory of inability to exceed the speed of light using extrapolation.

While it has turned out to be a truth, that one cannot exceed the velocity of light, the reasoning he used seems to be faulty unless he was aware, or subconsciously knew, that the speed of light is dependent on the nature of vacuum and the means that accelerates a body is limited by the nature of the medium and its ability not to exceed the speed of light especially when burdened by a body of mass such as a particle. Waves in the vacuum can only travel at the speed of light if unburdened by a mass. The wave velocity that drives a body will be reduced in proportion to the amount of mass that it is driving.

A rocket engine creates waves that push the rocket ship but the waves can only travel in the medium that creates the wave while burdened by the mass of the ship. If there were a way to reduce the inertia in which the ship is traveling, by creation of a vacuum comprised of smaller particles, called tachyons, the rocket engine creating waves that are in a more dense medium will have a chance of driving the ship faster, perhaps beyond the speed of light as measured in the inertial frame being left behind. A vacuum behind or emitted as denser particles will create more power but perhaps not more speed.

Because the vacuum is a particle medium, the same problems will likely exist that exceeding the speed of sound faces, an increase in the density of air built up due to the speed of the ship pushing the particles together to increase the density of air ahead of the ship. Decreasing the angle of attack relative to the direction of movement by the shape of the ship is limited in help so long as the ship has volume. The problems of resistance due to buildup of density is reduced when only in vacuum but if a means could be devised to reduce the density buildup in air, then speed that exceeds the speed and breaking the sound barrier and the sonic boom it creates might make travel beyond the speed of sound be more common.

Perhaps a vacuum pump that pulls the molecules of air into a sideways exhaust would do the trick. If the existence of the vacuum were to be acknowledged, a way to manage vacuum might be a possibility. Locating a region of travel in which the density of vacuum is less, such as locating an entanglement path would allow speeds faster than our light will travel. It may be that this is a discussion involving creation of a tachyon field, a field of smaller particles in the field, if theoretically created, there is a chance that an instability would expand to disturb the entire structure of reality and therefore considered unstable, but unlikely.

The tachyon field is a true scientific theory though not having been created in reality. The tachyon particle is one that is perhaps smaller than those comprising the vacuum but the vacuum as described herein of an infinite size range, there can be no tachyon smaller than all particles in the vacuum.

The protons and neutrons comprising the nucleus of Hydrogen atoms are understood to be made of quarks where neutrons basically have an inactive or very limited surrounding magnetic field. The main known differences between these two particles is that one quark is somewhat different in one compared to the other causing them to behave differently. There are other particles that are smaller but most likely infinitely large compared to the largest particles comprising the vacuum, perhaps making them comparable to the water in chemical experiments.

If the vacuum is made of particles and they too must be surrounded by a gradient or field of what must be to them much like the vacuum is to the known particles, comprised of infinitesimally small particles with fields of their own. Those fields must be made of particles also having gradient fields of relatively infinitesimal particles and so on such that the sizes of particles in the vacuum and perhaps throughout the entire universe are infinitely variable. This arrangement allows the vacuum to be able to behave as vacuum, even to mimic empty space by having no frictional forces due to lubricating qualities of the infinitely small particles that separate all the known masses.

While discussing the vacuum and the particles of known masses, we are discussing the very matter that the brain is comprised. Furthermore, this discussion is based on the concepts of mechanical causation which is missing from the modern theoretical physics where causation has been largely, if not totally, deleted from the physics of matter at the level of the particles. Therefore, as described here, nothing herein contravenes anything that is set out in theory, but on the contrary, is intended to support all or mostly all that is described behaviors in current theory.

Electromagnetic waves of physics are presumed to exist in empty vacuum and therefore thought must be comprised of particles, the photon particles, arranged in the familiar sinusoidal shape while passing through the vacuum. The material vacuum described here can form compression waves by deformation of their gradient fields while the cores are allowed to come closer together comprising a very dense space, dense enough to be mistaken for particles. No such waves are conceivable to theorists who are constrained to regard the vacuum as empty space. The cores that are pressed together in the peak region of a wave are undoubtedly of various sizes.

A wire with current under a potential will leak some of its internal magnetic properties outside of the wire itself even when insulated. The outside surrounding field can be captured by winding the wire in a tight coil around a magnet, a metal bar or even empty space to create a field at the ends of the winding. These external fields may be tested for current within the nerve fiber but whether it is actually used is beside the point. These fields are evidence of what is taking place within and it is not electrons leaking out from the circuit but vacuum having particular properties.

What is being advocated herein involves a very simple adjustment that accommodates the existence of material vacuum and its properties with theories based on the mechanics and wave content rather than just electrical current that is being found. An embedded message in long carrier waves is an old science that has not been reported to be contained in brainwaves. Radio and television information is often transmitted on top of carrier waves   that are likely the same electromagnetic waves detected in EEG examinations of the brain but perhaps on a weaker scale, and they may be found to be intelligible such as complete images that were accepted by one or another sensory organ some day as technology advances.

New methods may be needed for testing waves for hidden information beyond wavelengths, needed to understand what is happening in the brain. If current is created at a sensory organ then content may differ depending on the source. A wave created by sound will have a different quality than one containing visual information. If these are broadcast throughout the brain cavity, different parts of the brain may recognize the source as something it needs to complete a logic analysis.

Attributing electrical current to moving electrons will not produce a significant result and electrons flowing through complex biochemical material would not likely be allowed, evolutionary wise. If current is electron flow, then the atoms that lose the electrons should be free radicals.

To allow atoms to collect memory, rather than follow the electrons modeled as in orbit, the atoms must be constructed by addition of whole Hydrogen atoms intact and functioning as layers or in shells contained in the nucleus with the electrons facing outward or inward for inner layers under the outer valence shell. Though chemically inactive, they may be active while still maintaining their magnetic envelope of the proton, may be able to augment the outer valence shell Hydrogen atoms, facilitating storage of information as memory images.

Otherwise, the behavior of the electrons can follow the behavior as set out in the periodic tables of the elements where only the outer shell can be active in chemical reactions as the valence shell. The magnetic lines of force, the Faraday tubes, will likely extend beyond the location of the electron to the extent that a magnetic field can be measured as an extension of the proton envelope able to collect waves in the atmosphere striking it from every direction to be passed down towards the proton core.

The electrons, theoretically each act alone in the process being described theoretically as emitting photons and responsively changing orbitals according to quantum mechanics without a mechanical model to support both in maintaining a supply of photons for emission or the orbit and orbitals when reading the waves that come its way.

Wave energy may be theoretically stored in the

atoms in the form of a pulse and that subsequently an amount of energy is emitted in another wave having a slightly different form of light waves. The energy in orbits that can be mathematically calculated to coordinate with the light waves that are detectable gives some credence to internal processes capable of performing the observed tasks but no certainty can be established regarding the particular structures that are being accepted in the theoretical models. Theory places proton alone in the nucleus acting as a point charge somehow directing electrons in orbit.

The sensory apparatus captures a section of a spherical wave and sends it directly to a specialized lobe beneath the CORTEX where it is processed and sent to the outer surface of the CORTEX for logic processing. A waves are captured in the extensions of the envelope that are the Faraday tubes or magnetic lines of force and must immediately form an envelope around the wave which preserves the wave. The particles in the envelope may attract vacuum particles, particle by particle, outside the wave envelope forming an exact clone of the original wave. The copy is then emitted as a wave causing the atom to begin to rotate as each quantum wave is copied causing the sinusoidal shape of the clone as an electromagnetic wave.

DARK MATTER MECHANICS

The proton envelope is a magnetic gradient that was originally construed as a collection of Faraday's magnetic lines of force that can extend out into the atmosphere where the magnetic forces are measurable. Einstein sought to explain the behavior in empty vacuum in his field theory, as a mathematical phenomenon. With Einstein's empty space, the mathematical technique for describing behavior has been adopted today while dropping cause and effect of physics and especially mechanical causation such as being developed herein.

While the lines of force are and extension of the proton's envelope that reaches out into space, the electron must remain close to the proton in the nucleus where the emission of waves may take place. To conform to theory, the electron is forced to move away from its former position according to the quantum mechanical model due to changes by wave capture within the envelope. The magnetic line of force, as an extension of the proton envelope, can capture electromagnetic waves very effectively by acting as an antenna, with the ability to pass captured waves down the envelope toward the core proton and perhaps copy internal structures using outside material as a means of wave emission. The copy must reflect the change in size of the envelope just as the electron does.

MEMORY, MIND AND CONSCIOUSNESS

During the traversal down the extended proton envelope due to gradients in the vacuum, certain changes are known to theoretically take place in gradients whether or not acceleration actually takes place due solely to the gradient effects. Gravity is a measure of acceleration and magnetic fields are similar structure that is also acceleration according to experimental results and Einstein's special theory of relativity. The magnetic field is a changing inertial frame of its own causing length contraction that flattens particles of matter and can for normal particles cause increases in mass.

Changes must take place due to changes in the vacuum atmosphere that is the same as change in the inertial frame that waves find themselves and effects of acceleration at the same time. The wave is comprised primarily of vacuum cores pressed close together during the wave peak formation with their gradient field largely stripped away and left behind. It is likely the frequency of wave peaks that contain information and frequencies must be stored, if so., separated by troughs.

Compression algorithms in computer science vary but the type must be acknowledged when decompressed. Sensory organs extract an area from the spherical waves and detect motion as layers of information as spheres within spheres are received with each layer representing a time difference. These are sent to a specialized part of the brain for processing for detection of beginnings and ends of motion containing gray matter for logic, perhaps creating a carrier wave studded with information waves and sent to the main CORTEX to integrate the information with other sensory inputs.

Compression is undoubtedly a process of comparing the images with immediate and long ago past images using neural network logic. A timestamp would allow synchronization to other sensed information from other organs and an identifier for the source, if known. We each know the capabilities of our brain and knowing it may be a product of the vacuum may allow us to better comprehend its capabilities. Apparently, we each have different means of organizing memories.

Waves that are allowed into the proton envelope are already compressed due to reduction in their gradient structures during wave creation. The cores alone may identify the wave structure able to be decompressed by means of infusion of gradient material perhaps by entangled channels infusing small vacuum particles to copy the original gradient field, copying and lifting the waves into a higher location out of the envelope and into a Faraday tube, a line of force extension of the envelope, and into a logic structure to be analyzed for relevance to current situations that may exist or for use in the imagination where bits and pieces are used. Past memory is used in making plans for the future so it is likely to be regularly called upon.

Theoretical physics seeks to analyze unseen behavior by using rules constructed in experimental physics, presuming that they are relevant in what may be a far different atmosphere than that in which the rules were formulated. The brain presents a far different use of rules or violation of rules and the exact methods and processes may not be accessible due to limitations in our personal logic systems.

Infinite memory storage seems possible in the infinite space we live in but memories do get lost at times or after long lengths of time by processes that must be abnormal. Some of us remember events along with dates and surrounding contexts while others lack that ability to some extent evidencing differences in logic systems from individual to individual.

Waves can only be preserved if the particles are glued together somehow or else they will simply dissipate into the surrounding atmosphere. A wave forms a group envelope to save the integrity of the wave as it passes down the gradient toward the relatively great mass of the proton core particle. Because each wave is an entire image, perhaps of an entire set of sequenced images, processing is minimal if unlimited storage is available. Perhaps the information contained herein may allow each of use to analyze our own logic in regard to memory storage and recall with knowledge that we each have unlimited storage ability if we decide to use it since memories stored in many places are more likely to be recalled as thoughts or sensed..

It should first be noted that the work contained herein has been dependent on the findings of physics and theoretical physics where assumptions are made in the effort to discover the underlying causes of behavior found in those two sciences. Understanding that models in theory are not complete representations of all that occurs in a context of a discovery or the credibility of the theory relied upon in new discoveries that may be outdated or unlikely to be founded on reliable data.

The End

www.ingramcontent.com/pod-product-compliance
Lightning Source LLC
Chambersburg PA
CBHW021811170526
45157CB00007B/2535